MANAGING INNOVATION

ABOUT THE AUTHORS

N.S. SREENIVASAN, after obtaining his Masters Degree in Statistics from the University of Mysore, joined SQC and OR Division of the Indian Statistical Institute in 1956. He was extensively involved in consulting work related to Management of Quality in a large number of industrial as well as service organisations like hospital, transport.

In 1975, he joined M/s IDL Chemicals Ltd. He had several key assignments as Manager (QC), Manager (Safety), Production Manager, Works Manager, Chief Executive of the explosives manufacturing unit at Rourkela and now General Manager (Planning, Research and Development).

He has published a number of papers on diverse subjects like Quality, Safety, Personnel, Innovation and General Management in a number of national and international journals. His book on 'Management of Safety — Concepts and Tasks' published in 1984 has very well been received and had an extremely favourable review from several national and international journals. He is a founder-member of Indian Association for Quality and Reliability and an active member of Quality Circle Forum of India, Hyderabad Chapter.

V. NARAYANA after obtaining Master's degree in Statistics from the University of Mysore, joined the Statistical Quality Control and Operations Research Division of the Indian Statistical Institute in 1956. Since then he has been involved in promotion training and consultancy in applications of Quality Management and SQC techniques in a number of different types of industries — Engineering, Pharmaceuticals, Textiles etc.

He has been guest faculty at programmes organised by Administrative Staff College of India, Engineering Staff College of India, National Institute for Small Industry Extension Training, Jawaharlal Nehru Technological University etc.

He is a founder member of the Indian Association for Quality & Reliability and Quality Circle Forum of India.

MANAGING INNOVATION

CONCEPTS AND TASKS

N.S. SREENIVASAN
General Manager (R&D & Plng.)
IDL Chemicals Limited
Secunderabad

V. NARAYANA
Senior Specialist
Indian Statistical Institute
Hyderabad

CONCEPT PUBLISHING COMPANY, NEW DELHI 110059

ISBN 81-7022-443-8

First Published 1992

Published and Printed by
Ashok Kumar Mittal
Concept Publishing Company
A/15-16, Commercial Block, Mohan Garden
NEW DELHI 110059 (India)

Lasertypeset by
Microtech Advance Printing Systems (Pvt.) Ltd.
H-13, Bali Nagar,
NEW DELHI 110015

Dedicated to
The Sacred Memory of their Parents
Seethamma Iyengar and Sundara Raja Iyengar
Subbalaxmi and Venkata Krishnaiah

PREFACE

Individuals age, decay and die. This is the cycle of life. No one can escape the inevitable end. But, an institution need not be a prisoner of this cycle of life. An institution can be old but not aged; an institution can ever grow without fading. To accomplish this an institution has to be managed for tomorrow using "innovation" as a key result area.

An institution thus managed for the future would always be geared up to

– meet the newer needs and services of customers;
– identify newer customers for existing products and services;
– avoid utilising the resources to defend yesterday;
– exploit the newer opportunities to grow;
– arrest/minimise the effects of emerging threats, if any.

Such an institution, no matter how old it is, would remain young and energetic through always being socially meaningful and economically profitable.

The importance of innovation in the present context can be gauged through the words of Tom Peters "Get innovative or get dead". Innovation is not just R&D; not mere science and technology; not necessarily an original idea; not required to be an invention or discovery; not mere improvement and need not be always dependent on new knowledge, high investment or sophisticated technology. Then, what innovation is, what are the characteristics of innovation process: How innovation is to be organised; what organisational features promote its growth; which ones stifle it? A clear understanding of these important basic issues holds the key to organise and strengthen innovation activities in an institution. Without such an understanding, innovation cannot be effectively organised as an on-going result oriented activity. The purpose of this book is to create a proper understanding on all the basic issues related to innovation so that industrial enterprises could organise and strengthen innovation as a business venture.

The great works of Drucker, Toffler and Tom Peters have inspired us immensely. The nature of help derived has been clearly spelt in a separate note covered under Bibliography.

We have been immensely benefited through the hands-on experience gained through their association with SQC and OR Division of Indian Statistical Institute and M/s IDL Chemicals Ltd. The later one needs a special mention. It gave one of us the privilege to conduct an in-plant programme on 'managing innovation'. The favourable enthusiastic reaction to this programme gave an indication that a book on basics of managing innovation would be of immense value to institutions and managerial personnel. Thus M/s IDL Chemicals Ltd is at the root of this book venture and it is gratefully acknowledged. In the company, we are indebted to Dr. E.G. Mahadevan, Managing Director for his towering inspiration, and encouragement; Shri B.C. Pati VP(O) and Shri R. Vedam, General Manager (Rtd.) for all their immense help and support.

Views expressed in the book are those of only the authors and they do hope that the book would be well received and utilised by the industrial enterprises as well as managerial personnel.

N.S. Sreenivasan
V. Narayana

CONTENTS

LIST OF EXHIBITS

1

AN OVERVIEW: Why Innovation

Current Scenario

Kinetic landscape envelops the present society. Break-up-of-the old rules is central to this kinetic situation. "Change" is its one word description. Concepts, techniques, approaches, systems and procedures which helped to manage efficiently many an enterprise facilitating them to grow and stay prosperous over the years are no longer effective.

Changes have always been there. Progress is in fact symbolised by changes. What is of relevance in the present context is not just the change but its constituent elements of surprise, suddenness, velocity; and the fact that such a change embraces every activity of the society rocking its very foundations. Few examples given in Exhibit 1.1 illustrate these points.

Relevance of the Past

Strategy of war and weaponry which helped to win many a battle in the past can prove to be disastrous under changed circumstances. This has been the case with respect to managing institutions. Rule book and decisions by the rule book both of which served well all these years in the effective management of several institutions are no longer valid to cope up with the present-day problems marked by change and turbulence.

Under conditions of change characterised by surprise, suddenness and high velocity, the past experience would become increasingly less and less relevant and effective to meet the needs of the day. Past experience, approach, practice and systems would not help to solve the current problems as past by itself, is getting grossly out of focus with the needs of the day. Past not being able to guide the future is the current dilemma facing bureaucracy, political systems, industrial management and other social institutions. Ineffectiveness in handling problems facing the society is largely attributed to this dilemma.

Therefore, a high degree of "future consciousness" is what is needed now in the management of any enterprise.

Future Consciousness

Future consciousness is a state where past is used as a source of inspiration; vision is focused on to weave future developments and comprehend the challenges ahead; wisdom is energised to develop suitable sound concepts; objective is to develop organisational resilience and adaptability to surmount the challenges.

Today's society is a society of institutions. Therefore, society's prosperity rests on efficient functioning of its institutions. Efficiency and effectiveness of managing the present-day institutions rest on the institutions being driven by "Future Consciousness". This is manifested through management of surprise and innovation.

Management of Surprise and Innovation

Management of Surprise is a concept based on knowledge and intuition, wisdom and vision. It concerns with continuous scanning of the total environment: economic, social, political, cultural, technical, market etc. The purpose is to identify in advance the developments favourable and also unfavourable; use the favourable ones to the advantage of the enterprise; unfavourable ones to stem and/or minimise their ill effects on the enterprise. Thus, for instance 50s heralded the era of nationalisation of road transport. TVS, a well known enterprise of the time in road transport, saw the writing on the wall; diversified in time to manufacture automobile accessories wherein it had enough market knowledge. Today it is an ever growing organisation and is a leader in automobile accessories. There were also many other well-known road transport companies at the time. They failed to take cognizance of nationalisation or thought it fit to stall it. These are now either faded out or stunted beyond recognition. Entry of ITC into hotel industry as Welcome Group, is yet another notable example; a result of ITC having identified hotel industry a decade ago as a fertile area of investment and diversification.

Enterprises that are adaptive can take full advantage of the lessons of environmental scanning. Adaptiveness is reflected through innovative ability. Thus, innovation is the back-up force for management of surprise. Therefore, in future, industrial organisations that manage innovation effectively can only hope to survive well. Managing innovation is going to be a key-result area for top management.

It is an uphill task. The typical situation prevailing at present in the management of innovation indicates the challenges involved in organising innovation as a key-result area. These are discussed in the next chapter.

EXHIBIT 1.1

Change and Turbulence : A Few Examples

Fragmentation

1. Social, economic, political and regional forces emphasize distinct traits, differentiating patterns and distinguishing characteristics of different sub-groups within a group and different groups within a population to keep the identity of sub-groups. Hence, society and institutions move towards decentralization, segmentation and fragmentation. To find unity in diversity in this situation, is an intellectual challenge and demands social sagacity of a high order.
2. Regional pride, love of regional language, regional aspirations quickly spring-up and organise themselves fast into a formidable political force dislodging the well organised and deeply entrenched ones of the ealier years. This demands of the society competence, values of life and statemanship of the highest order to ably manage the contradictions without compromising on the basics; national unity, integrity and interests.

Industry — No Exception

3. The impact of fragmentation is felt in every area of activity — health, education, industry, employment, economic development. For example, the prevailing mass consumption consumer market breaks-up into tiny bits each having its own poroblems, expectations and rewards. Modern technology makes it possible to achieve customer-tailored production and thus cater to the needs of the fragmented tiny markets.
4. Industrial enterprises, which owe their present-day prosperity to mass production with high degree of standardization have to recognise that in the future the company that knows how to destandardize effectively may prove victor and resort to custom-oriented production catering to multiple standards even within the same product.

Change of Scale

5. The technology of miniaturisation and computer aided engineering system has shrunk the length of cycle-time of design-to-manufacture. This has brought in small size factories retaining all the versatile volume-variety features of "BIG" ones coupled with competitive quality and customer service. A clear trend of "BIG" being increasingly edged out by the small is seen.
6. The time-honoured attributes of "BIG" namely. Big is economical efficient and innovative, are being questioned. There is increased evidence to doubt whether at all big was efficient, economical and innovative. There is increased realisation that obsession with "BIG" has led many an enterprise to ignore/neglect good innovative opportunities only to regret it later. The classical example is that of Sony having bought at a ridiculous sum the licence for the new transistor from Bell labs and capturing the radio market all over the world.
7. Rate of obsolescence would be high at a level never before witnessed in any field. This itself will bring forth new problems. For an industry this means on the one hand few "anchor" products and fewer anchor technology – the ones that remain stable and unchanged over a period of time; and on the other facing many hitherto not handled, unknown, new and distinct problems. Some of these are need for new projects; infusing new class of workmen who detest routine but thrive on change, ambiguity and flexibility in work place unlike the present class wedded to standardized routine work schedule; and consequential organisational problems arising out of the co-existence of the old and new set-up with distinctly different work-ethos and value-scale.

Unification Trend

8. Across the international borders there would be an increased move towards unification. This process is already seen in areas of pollution, ecology, environmental control, trade and development. Institutions like EEC, UNCTAD symbolize this trend towards unification.

Consumer Force

9. There would be increased pressure towards making decisions democratically by informal citizens. This is already in evidence. Thus for example, assurance of atomic scientists and nuclear engineers on the safety of nuclear energy is no longer accepted at face value. They have to share facts and information. Likewise, many projects are held up under enviornmentalists' pressure.
10. Consumer movement by itself undergoes a sea of change; from mere economic goal to one of achieving a "saner, more civilized society and not necessarily a richer one"; from only issues on quality and safety to the complex one of "quality of life"; from a narrow focus on manufacturing industry to wider area of service; transport, communication, health, power, education etc.
11. Consumer movement will not be a monolithic unitary force but an assemblage of several ones each having its own chain of command, ideology, approach and proximity to power centres. Their growing strength and influence is felt even in our country at present. It will be a force to reckon with. It can reverse the decisions taken. Prominent examples are Silent Valley Project, raging controversy on Narmada and Tehri development projects.
12. Consumer gets importance through new legislative measures. Recent Consumer Protection Bill and amending even other acts give far reaching rights to consumer and put power into the hands of consumer. As far as consumer is concerned Private and Public Sectors' distinction does not exist. For example the act referred to above is equally applicable to Government run utilities such as Telephone Department or Electricity Board.
13. Laws and their judicial interpretation at one time helped growth of commerce and industry without inhibitions of product quality and safety. Courts currently view it as their duty to make it clear that "shoddy work does not pay". More fundamental amendments and enactment of laws are on the basis that law grows "out of the social reality and facts, not principles written on stone-tablets". Judicial pronouncements concerning quality and safety have far reaching consequences, as can be seen from recent trend-setting judgments.

Adaptation

14. Quick adaptation to changing needs determines survival. The game of cricket is a shining example. Imperial feudal origin, leisurely and fading out game that cricket was, has bounced back to its never-before-attained position through "one-day-international" and now it is not a mere sports. But it is a flourishing business, unification force and an entertainment for the masses.
15. It is recognised in information theory that with every relay in the communication system, "message" gets halved and "noise" gets doubled. This holds good for every level of organisation heirarchy and therefore, for efficient management of an enterprise under conditions of turbulent change, orgainsational structure has to be lean with few layers of heirarchy. This is leading to dismantling of heirarchical structure and bureaucratic system; to stay foremost in business three-layer heirarchy is already becoming a common feature.

2

INNOVATION – TYPICAL SITUATION: An Analysis

Typical Situation

A typical picture of how innovation is being managed is summarised in this chapter. Most of these traits can be found in varying intensity in any industrial enterprise.

- Innovation and R&D are synonymous. Hence, managing innovation is taken as managing R&D. Thus, innovation is not a company-wide activity but a departmental one.
- Involvement of production, quality control, marketing and sales departments in the selection of projects is minimal. They are involved/consulted when R&D deems it fit to do so.
- Majority of the suggestions of R&D are found impracticable and fail. Result is a waste of efforts, time and resources.
- There is a plethora of abandoned projects and products; and the idleness of related equipment and facilities; all these being an evidence of wasted resources, half-hearted attempts, ill-conceived projects or misdirected efforts.
- Investment decisions in R&D are primarily to derive tax relief/benefits.
- Patents registered have remained on paper; techniques developed are yet to be adopted; new products not finding market-acceptance, few new ones taken to market re-called/ withdrawn; all indicating that the approach is neither customer-focused nor market-driven.
- Management controls are not tooled to suit innovation activities. There is no specific policy, direction, guidelines on innovation activity. This has lead to drifting; taking up jobs which could best be left to "shop" to solve.

- Different functional groups are allergic to try new ideas. Any new idea from R&D evokes the comment "here comes yet another bug".
- Innovation in different functional areas like finance, industrial relations, marketing, distribution etc., are conspicuous by their absence.

A Paradox

This typical much-to be-desired-status of management of innovation is in stark contrast to what the industry as a class by itself has achieved over the years in terms of growth, expansion, diversification, updating of technology, acquiring new technology, profitability etc. What does this paradox imply? Does it mean innovation is of no relevance to the industrial prosperity? Does it imply industrial progress can be achieved in spite of not being innovative? or Does the contrast mean inability to manage innovation well? It is none of these things but neglect of innovation. It reflects dire need for attitudinal and conceptual changes for the better to manage innovation. Consequences of these costly lapses will be felt much later. Sins of father visit the sons. This for example, is reflected in the present plight of the country's oldest industry, Cotton Textile.

Thus in the context of Managing Innovation the following points need to be recognised:

a. Industrial boom will not there to stay for ever.
b. Industrial gowth can be sustained only through constant innovation.
c. Taking advantage of only the prevailing market conditions (without the action to sustain it through innovation) means in retrospect that the present is being managed efficiently well for obsolescence.

Pointer

Thus Managing Innovation assumes greater significance now than never before and it is not going to be an easy task. It calls for proper understanding of the meaning of innovation and what it is not; deeper appreciation of the innovation process and its peculiarities; recognition of the core points that constitute an innovative culture;

adoption of organisational practices that promote and sustain innovative culture; role of top management in giving the right direction, focus and facilities to have enduring innovation. These are some of the topics that are covered in this book on *Managing Innovation*.

Conclusion

Individuals age, decay and die. It is life. This is not true of institutions. They can be old but not aged; ever grow and not fade. This happens when institutions are managed well through :

– gearing up to meet newer needs and services of customers;
– not wasting resources to defend yesterday's products;
– recognising the significance of changes in the environment well in advance.
– taking advantages of the opportunities such changes may have and
– adopting steps to avert their threats, if any.

This amounts to efficient "Management of Surprise" supported by ably managed innovation in its broad business sense. This can be accomplished through adopting the concepts and task discussed in this book.

An institution ably backed by innovation remains eternal by being always relevant and meaningful to society; and thus effectively ward off the dreaded disease of organisational progeria.

3

INNOVATION: Meaning

Innovation : Definition

Figure 3.1 represents progression of an idea into a physical entity as a product, process or service, "IT" for short. This path is often referred to as R&D, invention/discovery, improvement or innovation. This is erroneous and confusing.

"Idea" ⟶ "Invention" or "Discovery" ⟶ Process / Product / Service / "IT" (for short)

Fig. 3.1

Consider Fig. 3.2 wherein one more station "Market" is added.

Innovation (Business) Phase

"Idea" ⟶ Invention or Discovery ⟶ Process / Product / Service / (IT) ⟶ Market

R&D Phase (Creativity Phase)

Fig. 3.2

Figure 3.2 focuses the core point that "IT" is not an end in itself but has to reach the "market", stay there and make a social/economic dent. Path from "idea" to "IT" is "R&D Phase" and the one from "IT" to "Market" is "Innovation Phase". Thus it can be seen that where the "creativity phase" ends "innovation phase" commences. "Creative phase" generates novel ideas and innovation phase transforms these novel ideas into things tangible and useful-product, process or service to "market".

Therefore, for any IT to become innovation, it has to enter the market, stay there and make a social/economic impact. Otherwise, it can be anything but not innovation. "IT" need not necessarily be taken in the restricted sense of product, process or service but can relate to any functional area, finance, marketing, distribution etc. Likewise, Innovation is not restricted only to industry but to any institution- educational, health, transport, communications, etc.

Emphasis on "market" in no way undermines the importance of the "idea". On the other hand, it underscores the fact that an "idea" not reaching the market is only like "Gold-in-the-Mine". For example, Raman-effect venerated by mahrshies of science was till recently a gold-in-the-mine but no longer now with the advent of laser technology.

Thus creativity phase without linked to innovation phase would render the former aimless, innovation phase without the back-up of creativity would render innovation sterile.

Innovation — Other Dimensions

Many at one time or other would have played cricket, mostly one day matches. Thus there is nothing new, novel or original about "one day cricket" as an idea. But it was left to the entrepreneurship of Parker to turn it as an innovation through one-day-international that has come to stay in the "market" and achieved its social/economic impact. Other similar innovative examples of common knowledge are ESI Scheme, Hire Purchase System. Thus for any IT to become innovation, it is not necessary that IT should be original, new or novel; simple, ordinary or common one will do, provided "IT" impacts the market.

Cheap "Transistor" of Sony about two decades ago swept-off the "perfect" traditional valve-radios in America and likewise electronics, administered a rude shock to the precision-engineered, capital-intensive, mechanical-system watches of even the prestigious, world-renowned and age-old Swiss brands. Thus resources spent, perfection achieved on an IT are no guarantee of its continued presence in the market.

Conversely an IT cannot be labelled as innovation only on the strength of the resources spent on it; level of perfection built into it; degree of scientific thought and technological sophistication invested in it. These may aid IT to become an innovation but afford no guarantee; acid test is, IT should reach and stay in the market; and cause a dent in it.

Many improvements such as increasing production and productivity; cost reduction; reducing wastage and sub-standards etc. are achieved. All these would be innovation when their benefits reach the market and make a social/economic impact. Otherwise they are only improvements. This is not to undermine the importance of "Improvement" but to clearly distinguish it from "innovation".

An enterprise with a record of achievements through its internal improvement reflects its potential to be an innovative company but can't claim to be one unless the improvements achieved impact the market. Thus, to become truly innovative the first steps to master are the ability to achieve improvements and solve problems.

Improvement is "better and more"; Innovation is "new and different". "Improvement" is an activity that has its locus and impact within the organisation unlike "innovation" which has its locus within but impact outside it — market; and the impact is of economical and/or social significance.

Patents by themselves are not an innovation in spite of their scientific and technical profoundity, economics, and usage. But they do become one only when they impact the market.

Innovative Organisation – Indicators

Having defined innovation as an "IT" achieving a social/economic impact in market place, a few of the indicators of a truly innovative enterprise can be stated as hereunder :

- Organising innovation as a distinct and major task
- Creating an innovative culture
- Directing innovative efforts to achieve "new and different" and not mere improvements.
- Outcome of one's own innovation efforts leading to Establishing new enterprise/business, introducing altogether new products, creating new markets and creating new applications

– Adapting innovative approaches in all functions of an enterprise to mobilise finance, forge collaborations, reach customers fast; render newer and better services to customers etc.

As mentioned earlier, the task of converting an enterprise into an innovative one is not easy. It calls for a clear understanding of the peculiarities of innovation process; inter-relationship of the process with other functional areas such as quality, marketing, finance etc., organisational practices; time-dimension etc. These are covered in the subsequent chapters.

4

UNDERSTANDING OF INNOVATION PROCESS

Background

"Full many a flower is born to blush unseen and waste its sweetness on the desert air", this message of Thomas Gray is very apt for "ideas" and patents. They spring up in large number. But only a very few-trickle, compared to the initial crop-impact the market and turn out to be innovative ones. Rest of the ideas and patents whither away at various stages in their journey right from their conception to market.

As already noted in the previous chapter the path that innovation takes has four important stations – generating the idea; research to convert idea into invention/discovery; developing the "research" output as an "IT"; and establishing the "IT-in-market". The specific segment concerned with the task of taking the "IT to Market" is innovation activity. As a rule of thumb the ratio of expenditure at each of the four stations is of the order of 1 : 10: 100 : 1,000 to 10,000. This reflects the enormity of the cost of the "IT-in-Market" phase, the innovation activity. Thus an understanding of the characteristics of innovation process is a compelling economic necessity. If the characteristics of the innovation process are not understood it may lead to stiffling of the process itself resulting in huge waste of resources, effort, time and money. Some of the important characteristics of the innovation process are briefly dealt with in this chapter.

Characteristics

The characteristics of the innovation process are as follows and each one of these is briefly outlined:

(a) Synergy dependent
(b) Input of ideas – diverse sources
(c) Screening does not imply success
(d) Ultimate success – market impact
(e) "IT"-in-market not "IT" vs "market"
(f) "Near Success" – a camouflage for failure
(g) "Continue, do not abandon; break-through is round the corner", yet another camouflage for failure
(h) Cast the net wide
(i) Failure-know it well

(a) *Synergy – Dependent*

"IT" impacting the "Market" (economic/social) is innovation. It is the end result of a successful synthesis of diverse ideas and effective contribution of specialised functional groups. Thus it is no longer the commonly perceived activity located at a single-station "Research and Development" carried out by a single person or group of persons at that station.

Innovation activity in most of the cases is typically a process of rearranging with insight the inofrmation and knowledge available into new ideas and entrepreneurial opportunities. In such a process, two heads are better than one. Thus, if more minds are around a problem, it would bring further newer insights, better ideas, novel solutions. This is what Synergy-Dependent means. Thus innovation process is a highly synergy-dependent activity; working together of diverse agencies/people including ones like suppliers, customers and even external experts.

(b) *In-put of Ideas – Diverse Sources*

Ideas can come from totally different disciplines and diverse circumstances. Each one of these apparently appear to be totally disconnected with one another. Thus for example with the computer of 1946 none thought at the time the possibility of it being either in a wrist watch eclipsing the mechanical system or in the hand to wipe out the time-honoured slide-rule.

Another example is the debt – for nature swap conceived by Thomas Lovejoy and pioneered by World Wild-life Fund, USA (WWF-US) in 1984 as a new tool for leveraging conservation funds to save the biologically valuable areas easing external debt burdens of the Third World Nations. This innovation was the outcome of linking the diverse circumstances namely:

> Grave conditions of external debt in Third World Nations; co-existence of internal debt burden; existence of a high proportion of forests in the world's most debt burdened nations; clearing these forests for farm land, pasture land, mining and timber to raise resources to reduce debt burden; forest clearnace estimated at 75,000 acres a day; increased threat to ecology and environment; favourable conditions in the commercial debt/equity market; a number of debtor nations proposing debt for equity programmes through which they planned to redeem portions of their debt in local currency for use in commercial and industrial projects.

In 1987, WWF-US affiliated itself with Conservation International and Stanford University's Centre for Conservation Biology to help to protect the world's forests by buying discounted debts and then redeem their value for conservation, rather than industrial projects thereby dealing with both the debt and the environmental crisis-a case of economic and social impact. The first deal of debt-for-nature swap was struck in July 1987 with Bolivia.

(c) *Screening does not Imply Success*

Normally inventions/discoveries are screened. The ones with high pay-off potential enter innovation phase. Screening implies that the one chosen is a right area of innovation and such a decision is the outcome of a careful analysis and thought. This exercise by itself does not imply that oil would be struck.

(d) *Ultimate Success – Market Impact*

Successful laboratory trials; scaled up "large scale" trials; registration of patent and claims made therein do not constitute innovation. The acid test is "IT"-in-Market". Path of innovation from "IT" to "market" never runs smooth and straight.

It is borne out by common instances like claims made in patents proving to be disappointing; totally unanticipated problems thwarting commercial scale operations; factors ignored as insignificant causing a wreck in a technology – transfer excercise etc. Non-technology factors like economic, political, social, cultural reasons also have their decisive role in the success of an innovation. The concern that is being exercised now on nuclear power generation; huge multi-purpose river-valley projects; petro-chemical industries that pollute ozone atmosphere through chlorofluoro carbon pollution etc. are some of the examples where innovation activity has to face the external non-technology factors.

Thus, innovation phase is uncertain. It is full of surprises and set-backs.

(e) *"IT"-in-Market' not "IT" vs "Market"*

Innovation can be a success or failure. Success, if there is market impact; otherwise it is a failure. It is a common experience that when failure is encountered it is rationalised away as :

- Market failed to recongise "IT's" superiority/advantage; hence IT failed.
- Market accepted "IT" but failed due to lack of supply – support.
- Market conditions changed by the time "IT" arrived.

This rationalisation reflects compartmentalised approach to "IT" and "Market". The outcome of such a dichotomy has to be a failure. It should not cause a surprise. Such a dichotomy can run right through the entire process, albeit, unintentionally and without being even aware of it. Hence it is always necessary to recognise that innovation process is one of "IT" impacting the "market" and; the two, IT and Market, cannot be torn apart and treated as "IT" vs "market". Market-orientation and customer-driven approach to innovation will always focus the innovation efforts to meet market/consumer needs and no scope would be there to encounter failures of the types stated above.

(f) *"Near Success"*

When an "IT" fails to make the desired impact on the market, it is "Customary" to call it "Near Success". There is no such thing as near success. It is only success or failure, in the context of an innovation activity.

When a very successful product/service is imitated with certain changes, it may fail in the market in case the changes adopted were to go unnoticed and/or not accepted by the customers. Such failures are generally camouflaged as "Near Success".

There will be greater temptation to spend more resources to achieve success. Such a decision need to be taken with care and caution suppressing egoistic considerations. Otherwise it can lead to waste of resources.

(g) *"Continue, do not abandon; Break-through is round the corner"*

Innovation is business. Innovation means achieving economic success; making a social impact. Otherwise it is not an innovation activity. There cannot be innovation for the sake of innovation. It has to click in a reasonable time which can be realistically set.

If an innovation project fails to click in a reasonable time, reasons may be more than one and all necessarily may not be linked to persons involved with the project but could be even due to external factors. But the point to be noted is that a project that fails to click in a reasonable time should be abandoned and not continued as an innovation project.

Thus "continue, do not abandon" is yet another way of camouflaging a failure-situation which need to be identified, avoided and relevant points of learning value be recognised for future guidance and use.

At times, may be rare, "continue-do-not-abandon" can also be a deliberate move to cover up one's failure and gain time with the hope of rectifying it. Such cases will have a highly demoralising effect on the innovation activity as a whole. Hence as a rule it may be worthwhile abandoning all such cases after due scrutiny.

(h) *Cast the Net Wide*

Ideas are capricious; brilliant ones burn-out; feasible ones fail; ignored ones succeed. Hence mortality rate of ideas is high in R&D phase and higher still in innovation phase. Therefore enhancing the catchment area by increasing the number of experiments and experimenters improves the chances of success. The conventional "one-at-a-time" and/or "one-after-the-other" approaches to innovation are not conducive, productive and can prove to be costly in the long run.

(i) *Failure – Know it Well*

Failure in its entirety and diversity should be clearly understood. It is crucial to innovation's success. For example directing the efforts to understand several types of failures in a product including the ones due to its misuse or wrong use; and devising necessary measures to prevent them renders the product robust and reliable in market, enables it to stay there and impact the market.

Likewise recognising and understanding the parameters of "perceived quality" helps to build into the product/service those differentiations and distinctive features which are of value to the customer. This can help the innovated product/service make an impact on the customer/market and achieve innovation success.

Thus to summarise, it could be seen from a perusal of these different characteristics, the innovation process of taking "IT" to "Market" is elusive, slippeny, messy and an unpredictable one that never runs smooth. Such an understanding is basic and fundamental to build a congenial environment for innovation activity. It helps to integrate the innovation efforts effectively to achieve various demands on it in terms quality, safety, time-target etc.

Avoidable Angularities

There are a few human angularities which by themselves thwart innovation progress. Such angularities coupled with the very way-ward nature of the characteristics of the innovation process which have already been covered can spell disaster to an innovation project. Therefore, it is necessary to recognise these angularities which are of relevance to innovation activity and avoid them. Some of these are also dealt with. Consider the following few true-to-life case illustrations:

(a) In a manufacturing unit a certain suggestion is made to effect cost-reduction. The suggestion comes from an ordinary level not important enough in the bureaucratic hierarchy. It gets lost. Another suggestion comes up. It is of much lesser significance compared to the earlier one. But it originates from divisional head. All sit-up, think, accord priority and implement.

(b) A development project is taken up. Adequate efforts and reasources are spent. "IT, the end result of the project, is introduced in the market; reception found to be good. Scaling up runs into rough weather on grounds of certain facilities not being able to conform to statutory regulations. Such a conformance is vital but not found possible to comply with. Project is suspended. Innovation group stands to ridicule and the innovation activity gets its worst set-back.

(c) In a yet another product development exercise, the team comes out with a product technically superior to the contemporary ones. It is slated for introduction into the market. Marketing group offers certain suggestions to improve the customer-appeal and make it more user-friendly. Innovation group ignores them as of no consequence on the ground that they are basically nothing to do with technology and hence do not any more enhance the product's technological superiority. Technologically superior product is introduced in the market. "Ignorant" customers are unable to appreciate the technologically superior traits built into the product. Thus it fails to make a mark in the market place.

(d) "R&D" Department comes out with a new product. The concept behind it, advantages to be derived etc. are explained to manufacturing and marketing group. Certain practical problems and difficultires to be encountered are brought forth. Typical reaction; Well these are the problems of the "field" and as such they need to be solved by marketing or manufacturing. R&D, it does not have time to anticipate all these problems extraneous to it and find solutions to them. If done, it would only be diverting its attention to other areas leaving no time to concentrate on its respective field of study/specialisation. The "higherups" dismiss the views of manufacturing and marketing as excuses offered to cover up lack of concern and interest in the project. The end result, innovation work gets lost in the controversies.

The instances cited above are not uncommon. The end result of each instance is the same-failure of innovation project. But each has a different reason. These reasons need to be understood and appropriately remedied to improve the chances of success of an innovation project. These reasons for the sake of understanding fall into the following three different angularities : and each one is briefly dealt with:

(a) Perception problem
(b) Technical hubris and
(c) "Holy-Cow" situation

(a) *Perception Problem*

Perception is a powerful force. Right perception is very crucial and important. It is so powerful that having a positive perception even over an apparently inconvenient situation can work wonders. Boss assigns a very difficult task to his assistant. The latter looks upon it as a ploy used to liquidate him. In the process he gets demotivated and fails. There may be another case of success under similar circumstances due entirely to altogether a different perception that the assignment is an opportunity given to him to demonstrate his ability.

Thus the power of positive perception must come to play in assessing the merit and worth-whileness of any project, idea or suggestion; preference and priority should not be based on heirarchical position of person(s) sponsoring the project or closeness of the sponsorer to power centre.

Likewise bringing to bear the perception that innovation process by its nature has to have set-backs and failures before achieving success and therefore no blame can be straight away laid at the doors of innovation team, can mitigate the negative fallouts of a set-back situation. Yet another way to avoid wrong perception would be to build an environment wherein the innovation team can have the freedom to abandon a project with justification when expected results are not obtained within reasonable time without the risk of its competence being questioned.

Thus it has to be recognised that positive perception is a powerful tool to achieve success. Negative/wrong perception leads only to devastating results like encouraging a wrong cause/person, discouraging a right cause/person, demotivation, frustration, wastage of resources, defeatistic attitude, wrong decisions etc. only to state a few.

(b) *Technical Hubris*

Technical hubris means an arrogant attitude that technical superiority of the process, product and/or services alone that counts; and all else is secondary. Innovation activity infected with technical hubris tends to be contemptuous about anything that is not technological knowledge; anyone who is not a technological expert, and ignores what is of value to the customer but respects the one that is technically sophisticated. In short, innovation activity with technical hubris gets isolated from other functional areas to remain lonely and aloof; gets cock-eyed vision to look upon, for example, its sales force and consumers as ignorant and a source of interference.

Free flow of ideas and suggestions from market; information on the factors that satisfies customers as well as the ones that irritate them; knowledge of product performance at customer end are the invaluable inputs to innovation activity. In-flow of such an input must be ensured to render innovation project customer-oriented and thus achieve success. But technical hubris causes the blockade of the very arteries that furnish such a valuable market information. Therefore it should be consciously eleminated. Otherwise innovation process is bound to meet failure with certainty.

Innovators known to exhibit technical hubris turn out to be dead-wood fast; messengers of gloom and; frustration. They would have no good opinion on work and/or colleagues. Invariably they would be despised by the juniors; neglected by colleagues and if still tolerated, ignored by the top. Justifiable sense of pride like having the latest manufacturing equipment and process; best technical know-how of the industry; continued market growth etc can degenerate unintentionally into technical hubris and hence such a possible degradation must also be closely watched and set-right at the very early stage. All these point out to the need for total avoidance and elimination of this dreaded organisational arthiritis viz technical hubris.

(c) *Holy Cow Situation*

It is a common feature to observe that innovation activity by itself possesses an aura of reverence and distances itself from the common folk.

Traditionally also, a powerful feeling has been built that

innovation activity needs brilliance, ingenuity, flash of genius at a level not ordinarily to be found in any other functional area. It is a holy-cow.

One common but powerful feature contributing to the growth of and perpetuation of "Holy Cow" situation is that success stories of R&D and innovation rarely speak of the toil, tears and sweat; anxieties and apprehensions; setbacks and retreats suffered before reaching the point of success. After the success is achieved, the story that is always told is invariably on the pattern of the classical "falling of an apple", the flash of genius. This reinforces the "holy cow" theory. Conventional practice of studding R&D Department with persons of high academic attainments also lends added credence to look upon innovation as "Holy-Cow". All these points are meant not to underplay the role of intellect in innovation activity but to underscore that innovation is not intellect only but it is fashioning of the intellect to impact the market. Holy cow situation in its real terms emphasises "othodoxy" and "purity" of the disciplines involved; promotes isolation and compartmentalisation; leads to a state where R&D/Innovation exists for its own sake and not for market-impact. All these are the very anti-thesis of innovation activity. Hence, holy-cow situation is not conductive to innovation activity.

Holy-Cow situation, apart from imparting these wrong focus and mis-direction, engenders certain undersirable traits possibly unintentionally and even unconsciously. They are breeding egoism, individualism and an attitute of playing-close-to-one's-chest. All these inhibit synergy-development, so essential for the success of an innovation activity.

An antiodote for these is to look upon innovation as adventure which infact it is. Adventure is planting "flag-on-the-target". The attributes of an adventure are team work, anxiety, difficulties, heroism, pragmatism, retreat, round-about, rugged, setback. It is also highly technology dependent. All these hold good equally well for innovation activity. Hence innovation is adventure both in its intent and content. Therefore look upon innovation as adventure. It helps to eschew holy cow approach; avoid all its unfavourable fallouts and promotes synergy.

An Empirical Observation

The success rate in innovation activity is very low. This is due to the very nature of innovation process as well as the human angularities already discussed. It is of practical importance to note that on a very rough basis 10 per cent of the failure is due to unpredictable nature of the innovation process; 60 per cent to human angularities; and 30 per cent due to the interaction of the two.

This highlights the need for having positive perception, avoidance of technical hubris and holy-cow approach to innovation activity, if good progress is to be ensured.

Conclusion

In conclusion it can be stated that the path of innovation process by the very nature of its characteristics is uncertain, slippery and not smooth. To progress on such an uncertain and unpredictable path that innovation process is, it is important to eliminate the avoidable road-block in the shape of human angularities, namely perception problem, technical hubris and holy-cow situation. These are not merely road-blocks impeding the progress. They are vision-blinders. They have the power to consign the innovation activity to isolation, cutting it off from customer and market. They render innovation activity sterile. Hence they have to be eschewed.

5

TIME ELEMENT IN INNOVATION ACTIVITY

Innovation

The criteria of an innovation activity have already been discussed in the earlier chapter and these are summarised hereunder for providing continuity to the subject-matter of this chapter.

- Innovation is taking "IT-to-Market" and achieving market impact – social/economical.
- Innovation is business. Satisfying one's inner urge and/or intellectual curiosity do not constitute innovation activity. They are only incidental in an innovation activity.
- Market Impact is a tangible physical entity capable of being felt, seen, enjoyed and experienced by the customers.
- Customers in the context of innovation are external to the company.
- Improvements in production, productivity and efficiency, however impressive they may be within the company, cannot be innovations unless they make a direct impact on market.
- Innovation activity does not necessarily mean use of high technology, flash-of-genius, break-through ideas. Its attributes need not necessarily be one of involving huge cost, enormous effort or having faced great difficulties.
- Presence of any of the above inputs, individually or collectively, by itself cannot be an innovation; touch stone is market impact.
- Innovations can originate from ideas that are very simple, ordinary, nothing – novel, new or original about them.

The peculiarities and distinguishing features of innovation-process and the importance of their understanding have already been discussed in Chapter 4. This chapter also highlights the points related to achieve economy in "innovation-phase" whose cost is enormous compared to the one incurred up-to the "R&D Phase".

Time Dimension

There is one more dimension to the economics of innovation activity. It is time factor. There are two aspects of time dimension. First one is the actual time spent on innovation as such and the second one is actual time of market entry. The latter one is a matter of market intelligence and marketing strategy. Both are important.

Scope and Objective

Scope of this chapter is restricted to the first aspect of the time-dimension. The objective is to outline a few concepts and tasks related to time-management on the innovation project which help to hasten it and avoid delay.

Concepts and Tasks

Different concepts and tasks applicable to time-dimension of an innovation activity are as follows and each one is briefly outlined:

(a) Market-orientation and customer-focus
(b) Prefer "good" for "perfect"
(c) Pitch with lead users/lead suppliers
(d) "Non-Innovation" personnel – do not ignore
(e) Duplicate development approach – pays good dividends
(f) Infuse "Champion" culture and involve champions
(g) Small team approach, proves effective
(h) Debureaucratise, integrate
(i) Practice constructive impatience and ruthlessness

Market Orientation and Customer Focus

By the very definition of Innovation, it is known that it is an activity aimed at making a social and/or economic impact. Market impact is its main concern and objective. Hence innovation project must be market-oriented and customer-focused.

But it is generally construed as delivering a superbly desinged and engineered product/service; and consequently all the energies are directed towards this end.

It is to be noted that the real success lies in getting recognised as having delivered a superbly designed and engineered product at the hands of the customer. Instances are not few of many a superbly designed and engineered products/services having failed in the market place while the ones not perceived to be so by other manufacturers, sweeping the market dislodging the well established ones. "Nirma", "Good-Night", "QSS" are some of the recent exmaples in our own country. This highlights the fact that market-focus and customer-orientation provide right direction to an innovation project to achieve market impact. Thus, market-focus and customer-orientation make innovation activity productive, profitable and therefore time-wise effective.

This emphasis on market orientation is not to undermine the importance of superior design and engineering efforts. But it underscores the point that they should be subservient to customer's needs and market requirements, if the time and resources spent on an innovation project were not to go as waste.

Prefer "Good" for "Perfect"

In an innovation project, say a consumer product, it has to be recognised that the quality goal must be one of being superior to the prevailing national/international standards. Failing to recognise this and conforming to the prevailing standards would mean that mediocracy is built into the product and hence it is doomed to be edged out quality-wise sooner than later. In other words, the time spent on the project would be a wasteful one. Therefore, the product has to be better than the prevailing standards.

Besides this, the product/services must incorporate several of the seemingly simple, small, minor differentiations and features that are perceived as "valve" by customer – "Percevied quality characteristics". These quality considerations render the product/service truly customer-focussed and market-oriented.

Thus, defining "Good" as stated above, the "Perfect" can be thought of as:

"PERFECT" = "GOOD" + "EXTRA POLISH"

In reality, all the ingredients that come under "extra polish" are a source of waste of time and prolong the project unnecessarily. Thus, it is important to understand "perfect" pragmatically; avoid all wasteful "extra polish" and reach the market fast with a "Good" product/service. On a rough analysis 10-15 per cent of the time could be saved through avoiding "extra polish" provided one identifies them rightly in advance and weeds-out.

Pitch with Lead Users and Suppliers

Most of the consumers (users) and suppliers speak of the difficulties and problems of "yesterday", all the while feeling that they are tackling the current and future ones. Very few would decipher the future, anticipate the emerging trends and prepare in advance to seize the opportunities they ŏffer. Fewer still create the customer. The latter two categories constitute lead users/suppliers.

They can be identified through any of the following attributes :

- Know-how and process technology adopted is the latest
- Completely knowledgeable about the state-of-art and up-date the products and technology close to the state-of-art.
- Has wide product range and brings out new products/process/ services regularly
- Areas of application of products/services are also rich in variety
- Enjoy good-market-standing in terms of market-share, quality-reputation and service-to-customers
- Proven evidence of having gone out of the way to find solution to one's customers' problem
- Boyancy within the organisation exist to learn, acquire and implement the new
- Seek and seize any new opportunity for improving its image in the eyes of the customers.

Such lead users/suppliers need to be identified and one's own innovation project needs to be tied up with such lead users/suppliers. It helps to achieve success in a short time through organisational osmosis that sets-in through such an association. This is evident from the following :

(a) Many flourishing enterprises of today owe their pre-eminent position of the day to the entrepreneurial and innovative spirit they imbibed from the leading company while they were its one-time "small supplier".

(b) There are also instances of flourishing enterprises within the country founded by persons with high entrepreneurial and innovative ability – "lead persons" – who served at one time "big" institutions which could not match the talents and inner urge of the "lead persons".

"Non-innovation" Personnel – Do Not Ignore

Innovation means market penetration and impacting it. Market entry and impact have much wider implications today than never before. They are governed by numerous regulations and controls spread over several statutory agencies. They are to be cleared from "multiple windows", even before entering the market. All these can be a major source of delay.

Traditionally, tasks related to getting these clearances would be delegated to other departments and on their speed of action in getting such clearances rest the progress of the project. At times the delays suffered are too enormous to render the project itself lose its market significance. In more merciful cases project's significance as such may not be lost but cost-wise turns out to be prohibitive.

Therefore, the traditional practice of waiting to get clearances through faster action of the departments external to an innovation-project, must be given a go-bye. Instead those departments perceived as external, should be made a direct partner of the innovation activity to push the project. This calls for change in outlook simple, which if ignored, can be damaging to the very success of the project itself.

Duplicate Development Approach – Pays

Typical traditional cycle followed in an innovation project proposal is to set-up a committee; invite details of the proposal, make a rapid study of the "paper proposals"; review the specifications and then give a green signal for proceeding with the prototype. This cycle by itself would take a good deal of time, 20-24 weeks, in lucky ones. Proto-type is built. This would take another 20-24 weeks, if there is real "push" behind the venture. Otherwise the time taken would be much more. No prototype ever functions well and that too as per the levels anticipated. This is as is to be expected. But this natural expected outcome is lost sight off. Instead disappointment sets in. It looms large and gets intensified under the weight of the time, effort and resources spent already upto the prototype stage. The dreadful reality of the market changes that would have taken place by this time forces to re-examine and revalidate the relevance of the project itself. Under these circumstances the focus would divert itself to one of protecting the innovation project through salvaging it. At this stage the concern to avoid the "blame" for having taken up a project headed for failure energises the salvaging effort. Thus, the traditional approach has in it the built-in provision to cause delay, heart and waste resources.

Instead of this traditional approach, it is better to straight away "try ideas" through getting the requisite minimum resources for building a "hardware" in a short time of few months with the association of lead user and trying the hardware with him. At this stage lead user can even be an in-house department. In this approach of "trying the ideas" by building the "hardware" in a short time and trying it with a lead user, one could learn and understand the areas of deficiencies from customers' angle right from the beginning. This cycle if repeated in quick succession by building say two to three generation of prototypes, it would turn a version that is robust, reliable, user-friendly in a short period of time. The result is a product/service that is tested and proved before hand that has in it all the ingredients to make market – impact. The time taken by this approach is shorter than that in a traditional approach besides having a high assurance of success. Thus the duplicate development – approach pays good dividends.

Infuse "Champion" Culture and Involve Champions

As already pointed out in the earlier chapter, innovation activity is synergy-dependent and involves synthesis of diverse ideas. This call for an integrated inter-disciplinary approach. This is more so if the project were to be a Hi-tech one. Thus, technical competency is a must but not adequate. Potential benefits and promises that technical competency holds, yield results fast in an environment of "Champion Culture".

Champion culture can best be described by the following expression

F
Z E S T
D O
P

Each word of this expression symbolises the following characteristics of a champion-culture :

Z : Zeal, undying
E : Ego, Constructive
S : Spirit, Missionary
T : Tough
O : Optimistic
P : Passionate, Persuasive and Persistent
F : Fanatacism
D : Dedication

People create culture. In every organisation one finds technically competent personnel exhibiting the different ingredients of a champion culture as enumerated above in varying degrees. The right ones among them need to be chosen for an innovation project. Then the project will have a better chance of succeeding fast. The champion culture itself propels innovation activity fast to achieve success in a short time. It is not difficult to identify the champions. It only needs a thorough, objective, ruthless review of the track record of the competent persons the organisation has. If there is none, the organisation must not hesitate to bringing in persons from outside who are capable of building a champion-culture and develop champions fit to take up innovation project. The relevant point is to understand what constitutes a champion-culture in an organisation and recognise its crucial role in achieving rapid success in an innovation project.

Small Team Approach – Proves Effective

The phenomenal world-wide success in Quality-Circles in innumerable diverse areas manufacturing, marketing and service sectors like

Banking, Transport, Medical service, etc. prove the point that "small team" approach helps to move fast and achieve success. Innovation activity is no exception to this phenomenon no matter how massive the project may be.

If the project is huge, "Small within the big" principle holds good. It consists of logically breaking up the big-project into convenient well defined "bits"; each bit being in charge of a small team of champions; each team fulfilling its task well and in time; and integrating the efforts of each "bit" to bring out the "whole". The interface problems between the "bits" are easy to identify and solve. Thus, small team approach is equally effective in big projects as well.

The reasons for the success of a small-team can easily be realised and appreciated. In the first place, there is no "idle time" as being small means undermanned and hence had to work hard. Next the small team, would be like a "Circus" team characterised by no hierarchy, informality, free and open communication, perfect co-ordination, freedom of action, easy job-interchangeability, improvising and adopting the existing established methods/ideas/resources to achieve the "new and different" without wasting time to "discover the wheel"; and lastly a sense of ownership and commitment to the project are built into the team.

However, it is necessary to ensure certain ground rules while constituting the team. They are, the team must be small in size; essential disciplines like design, production, QC and marketing should compulsorily be in the team right from the start; every member of the team has to work whole time on the project – not part time and never in an "advisory capacity"; the leader chosen should be a "tinkerer", not a "blue-sky-dreamer".

Debureaucratise and Integrate

Bureaucracy means managing by "Rule Book"; decision based on "Rule Book", "Percedents"; taking decision at the "TOP"; handing it over to the hierarchical ladder to be implemented by its lowest rung. This works well in a familiar environment for known problems and routine activities. But it can cause disaster in a fast changing situation charged with new and different problems. The current times is a kinetic one which is beyond the capability of traditional bureaucracy to cope up, handle, solve the problems fast.

For this reason the organisational structure is undergoing a sea of change even in many of the successful industrial enterprises. Hitherto existing hierarchical pattern based on departmentalisation (segmentation) created islands of power and unwittingly nurtured well to guards of departmental interests (territory) instead of moving fast to achieve company's goals. Hence, the traditional bureaucratic hierarchy involving several steps is now crumbling and replaced by a horizontal one having just two or three steps to top focal-point.

Therefore, subjecting the innovation process which by its very nature is uncertain and never runs smooth besides being characterised by surprise, failure and disappointments, to a bureaucratic approach of procedures, clearances, approvals, etc. with the good intention of eliminating the uncertainties and streamlining the innovation activity proves counter productive; frustrates and stifles the innovation activity. In short, spells disaster as bureaucratic approach is not compatible to innovation process.

Therefore, planning for deliberate debureaucratisation is all the more necessary and important in handling an innovation project. In the traditional set-up the innovation process is linear and disconnected. Design is handed over to production engineering in turn to manufacturing and in turn to sales like a relay game. Each one in this linear relay chain feels that the "right" stuff was not received from the previous point. The result is a painfully slow progress of the project besides eruption of friction between the groups. This gets further accentuated by the human angularities already discussed in Chapter 4 ego, technical-hubris and "holy-cow" attitude.

Thus, bureaucratic approach to innovation no longer works and if adopted it does guarantee efforts but not results; ensures use of precious time and resources but not the returns commensurate with the resources invested. Use of small-team approach over comes the problems of bureaucratisation besides promoting synergy so essential for the success of an innovation project.

The approach to budgeting, accountability, evaluation of project potential etc. has to be on a different basis. For example, for innovation project budgetary aspects has to be assessed on the basis of what is needed and how soon it is needed? One has to actively look for anything that is missed out besides ensuring adequacy of the budget. The emphasis has to be on providing the minimum requisite and not cutting it down arbitrarily. Likewise, the organisational climate must be such that an infant in its R&D phase has to be protected from the issues that an "adult" has to face like estimated market potential, rate of return, payback period etc. By this approach, infants would survive and reach innovation phase and may succeed. Otherwise, many in R&D phase itself would die a premature death at the hands of traditional bureaucratic approach.

"Walk the talk". Debureaucratisation must be reflected in numerous tiny ways in daily chores while handling the matters concerning innovation. Persons engaged in innovation activity must feel and experience that there is no unnecessary bureaucratic interference on the one hand and on the other hold themselves fully accountable for the progress of a project or lack of it. In such an uninhibiting environment innovation project progresses fast. Unfavourable syndromes like "near success"; "continue, do not abandon, break-through is round the corner" which are a waste of time and resources get spotted early to take appropriate action.

Practice Constructive Impatience and Ruthlessness

To have impatience and practising it, are necessary and important for an innovation project-leader to avoid wasteful time. Thus, impatience is a virtue when used constructively. For impatience to be a constructive force, one has to listen and understand the views of others; assimilate the good points to strengthen one's own views to push the project. Thus, for example, commonly it is found in any discussion of a problem, about 60-70 per cent of time is spent on describing the problem, all the while perceiving it to be an exercise in finding a solution to the problem. Description is no solution and beyond a certain point it does not enhance or enrich the understanding of the problem. Hence, impatience has to be exercised in arresting waste of time when finding solution to the problem drifts to description.

Another source of delay is linking of events. Activities say A, B and C related to a certain event E are linked together and by which B could take place after A or C. Inter-linking implies delay. In reality 50 per cent of the activities that are linked, on close examination turns out to be illogical ones and delay due to linkage could have been avoided. Impose impatience to break the illogical linkages and thus avoid delay.

Yet another source of delay is misplaced attachment and crying over spilt milk. For example a proto-type is built. It does not work well. Costly errors are found; assumptions made prove wrong. Lot of effort is wasted. Time is lost. In a situation like this, natural feeling would be one of retriving the situation through salvaging and in unfortunate cases concentrating on "who was wrong". Both besides being a drain on time, are detrimental to innovation activity itself. One must be ruthless to discard the prototype; build a new one incorporating the lessons learnt out of the experience through an enquiring mind to learn from and understand "what went wrong". This keeps-up the tempo of innovation activity and saves time. Thus, constructive impatience and ruthlessness are close to each other. Their effective use in managing an innovation activity can save considerable time. They also help to prevent/avoid fraud.

Yet another source of delay is due to "hesitation" in changing a decision already taken. It is common that at a certain point of time decision already taken calls for a change, sometimes it may mean even a drastic but a necessary one. To arrest the time wasted over the wavering attitude which is "natural" for more than one reason, application of constructive impatience and ruthlessness prove useful and effective.

Conclusions

The above concepts and tasks related to effective utilisation of time spent in an innovation project cannot be arranged in the order of their importance. All are equally important and relevant. They are not absolutely independent but in fact interdependent. However, in a given project a few of the concepts may turn out to be more important and relevant than the rest. It depends on the organisational environment, project-team and its leader.

Efforts are not results. Hard work by itself may not yield results. But they do come, possibly with harder and smarter work. Concepts and tasks discussed here render the work behind a project harder, smarter and productive by better utilisation of time and avoidance of its wastage.

"Innovation is business" – achieving results of social and economic significance. In business, time dimension cannot be ignored. In conclusion, it can be stated that the different concepts and tasks discussed here help to efectively avoid wasteful time spent on an innovation project as such. The concepts are always to be kept in view and practised in day-to-day activity. They help to avoid the inherent dangers that delay can cause to an innovation project : rendering it totally irrelevant; degenerating the innovation project itself into one of a salvaging exercise.

6

INNOVATION AND QUALITY

Background

In the earlier chapters it has been noted that innovation activity means taking "IT" to "market" and achieving economic and/or social impact. In the context of the market impact, quality of "IT" – product, process or service – slated for the introduction plays a crucial role. Hence, a deeper and comprehensive understanding of the concepts related to achieving quality is vital and necessary for those involved in innovation activity. Against this background, some of the concepts of quality which are relevant to innovation are discussed in this chapter.

Quality Management

It is necessary to have an appreciation of what Quality management is and how it is organised in an enterprise known for quality reputation.

The current phase of quality management is aimed at having a self-sustaining and self-motivating approach to quality. This is a long haul from the traditional inspection-dominant-policing-activity that quality management was in the yester years. This metamorphosis has taken place through two intermediate phases namely SQC phase (Satistical Quality Control) and the subsequent TQC phase (Total Quality Control), the latter one giving quality management the role of an integrative, co-ordinating and unifying force.

Quality Management based on TQC has proved its effectiveness and achieved good results. Concepts and tasks of quality management found in common among the industrial enterprises known for their quality-reputation, entrepreneurship and innovativeness are as follows :

- A deep commitment to quality manifest through action and deeds
- Prevention of defects at source no matter what the source is
- Every specialised functional group in the organisation: Design, R&D, Purchase, Stores, Manufacturing, Maintenance, Quality Control, Personnel, Marketing, Customer services etc. discharging well its respective responsibilities related to quality.
- Treatment of causes of poor quality rather than their symptoms
- Control of quality by "operator" instead of controlling him for quality.
- Operational management being the king-pin in the task of achieving quality.
- Formulating quality systems and procedures as applicable to different specialised functional groups.

The above concepts are adopted in day-to-day activities through the following :

- Design review and control
- Vendor development and control
- Quality planning and co-ordination
- Quality maintenance by production centres;
- Field complaint analysis and follow-up;
- Quality training and motivation;
- Quality assurance in all areas : Vendor/Sub contracting; product identification, storage, packing and handling; manufacturing operations; measuring and test equipment; Design; Drawing change control etc.

Current Trends in Quality

The following are some of the trends regarding quality from consumers angle :

- Mass-consumption-consumer-market is fragmenting into tiny segments. Each segment has its own individuality, preferences, distinguishing characteristics. Therefore, any "IT" to make an impact has to fulfil the needs of each segment.
- Mass production to any number of pre-set-standards is possible through modern technology. Thus for example, an automatic

coffee vending machine can cater to multiple needs like only black coffee, black coffee with sugar, coffee with milk etc. Coffee vending machine is an ordinary equipment and not based on advanced sophisticated technology. Much more advance technologies are available which combine mass production features catering to manufacture to varying standards. Therefore, "custom production" to have "custom tailored" products on a large scale would be the order of the day.

- Quality is no longer a single dimension entity but a multiple one including safety, reliability etc.
- Consumer is gaining a strong hold. It covers not merely industrial, enterprises but also service institutions like, transport, health and communication etc.
- Legislation and laws are being increasingly enacted to protect conusmers' interest against poor quality. Judicial pronouncements concerning quality and safety have far reaching consequences including shutting down of the enterprises; shifting it from its present premises; compensation payable not linked to the injury suffered but the capacity of the enterprise to pay etc. In the light of these developments MNCs specially in the field chemicals and pharmaceuticals think twice before they decide to set-up their ventures or part with their knowhow.

The above-mentioned trends call for recognising new dimensions and perspectives on quality; integrate them as a part of innovation activity. Failing to do these would render the innovation activity out of focus on quality front and hence it may fail to impact the market. The new dimensions and perspectives on quality which need to be understood are dealt with in this chapter.

New Dimensions and Perspectives on Quality

Some of the new dimensions and perspectives on quality which are of relevance to innovation activity are summarised in Table 6.1 and each one of these is briefly dealt with.

Product Liability

Damages that one is liable to pay for the injury, accident or property-damage caused by the use of product because of a fault, defective or dangerous condition present in it is generally referred to as product liability.

TABLE 6.1: New Dimensions and Perspectives on Quality

Sl. No.	Concept	Tasks : Core thoughts covered
1.	Product-Liability	Do not shorten quality definition;
2.	Conformance to standard	Not a matter to feel jubilant, proud and get into blind alley.
3.	Perceived Quality	A power least exploited to reach "quality-peak"
4.	Customer complaints	"Complaints can be golden".
5.	Quality and Cost	Cost control may ruin quality; concentrate on revenue enhancement
6.	"Love of Product"	An under-utilised powerful emotion to achieve quality.

There are laws governing product-liability. Liability suits in advanced countries sound the death knell of industrial enterprises. There is also a move for enacting laws related to personal liability of engineers and technologists for product failures. Exporters to these countries should be conscious of product-liability laws. Developing countries are not lagging behind in enacting similar laws.

Quality is defined as "fitness for use". This definition is elegant, simple and practical. But against the back-drop of product liability, defining quality as fitness-for-use is a dangerously deceptive simplistic definition. It leads to keeping apart quality characteristics which comprise of only those that relate to visual, dimensional and functional parameters from the ones which have a bearing on product-liability namely safety paramters. These generally do not form a part of the conventional product-quality characteristics-package.

This neglect of safety parameters has been a major cause of many a failure of new product/processes in market place. Such a neglect has also sounded the death-knell of many an enterprise besides being a powerful source for enacting new legislative measures of far reaching consequences. Therefore in any innovation project specially the ones concerning products and processes, as a rule, it must be ensured that they must be fit-for-use-with-safety over its entire life. Otherwise risk of liability looms large. In daily work, vocabulary and practice, it is wise to note that there can be no quality without safety. An outline of the specific points related to product-liability that need to be taken note of in any innovation project are as follows:

a. Use of all the appropriate provisions of mandatory regulations, voluntary standards, national/international standards, industry customs in design of a product even though conformance to them is no guarantee against a liability suit.
b. Practice of collating, distributing and assimilating the information on new technology and processes; their ability to identify and eliminate the hitherto not possible hazards of a product.
c. "State of art" needs to be practised in design.
d. Analytical techniques like design audit check-list. Hazard analysis, failure-modes-and-effects analysis (FMEA), Fault-Tree-Analysis (FTA) etc. need to be adopted to identify weak spots, potential sources of trouble, trade off possibility etc.
e. Proto-type test and evaluation to confirm soundness of design consideration and claims.
f. Legal scrutiny and clearences of all the product promotional literature and documents regarding claims of the products in relation to qualtiy, safety and performance.
g. Updating of the practices to be in tune with the standard of quality, reliability, safety, unreasonably dangerous, defective etc. as expounded from time to time in judicial pronouncements in liability suits.

Conformance to Quality Standards

Generally product quality is expessed in terms of national or international standards. Conformance to any standards consistently is a measure of the minimum quality capability of a company.

Common reactions to this minimum level ability are as follows :

– Deriving high degree of satisfaction
– Taking pride in it
– A subject of major pronouncements of the company
– A focal point for wide publicity

This jubilant reaction does infact imply the following:

- Complimenting minimum quality capability
- Perpetuating minimum performance and mediocracy
- Complacency that can unitentionally lapse into inertia to reach peaks of quality performance and thus
- Ignoring opportunities of growth that peak-quality-capability affords to a company.

Thus setting the quality goal in any innovation project as one of meeting the national/international standards, means that it is condemned to mediocracy from the very start attendant with the obvious higher risk of being edged out quality-wise.

Hence in any innovation project specially related to product/processes the quality parameters chosen must be better and superior to the traditional levels and not merely meeting the national and international standards. In the ultimate analysis it is not the price but superior quality and customer service that achieve success in the market place.

Perceived Quality

The concept of perceived quality is best described through the words "beauty lies in beholder's eyes". This indicates a possible route to reach quality-peaks and avoid blind-alley noted earlier. It lies in continuously being aware of what gets registered in "beholders" eye, taking measures to incorporate them in the products and services offered.

In practical terms it consists of continuously getting

i. "SWOT" information on the product as assessed by consumers
ii. Ideas, suggestions and opinions from consumers over the numerous "Mini" differentiations and value additions that can be incorporated in products and services.
iii. Information as stated in (i) and (ii) with respect to the entire gamut of support-services rendered to consumers like billing, invoicing and document clearance; spares support; service after sales; solving consumer problems; training of consumer etc. and
iv. Utilising all the information thus obtained to supply product and services having in them the consumer-recognised

distinctiveness, differentiation and value-additions.

These help to maintain consumer-recognised edge over the competitors in respect of quality and services. There are many five-star hotels conforming to the same basic standards of quality and service; likewise many brands of TV; varieties of two wheelers etc. Inspite of conforming to same basic standards of quality, performance and service, only a few are at the "peak". Such peaks out of the equals are due to the power of "perceived quality", reality of building into product and services the consumer recognised parameters.

Thus having an up to date information on what constitutes perceived quality for a given innovation project and incorporating those features in the project enhances its success in the market place.

Methods of assessing perceived quality need to be formulated. There are not many in evidence. Hence developing appropriate methodologies to assess perceived quality by itself is a useful innovation project.

Customer Complaints

Customer complaints is a veritable source of ideas to improve quality and service. It also helps to set priorities. The uni-directional objective of an innovation project is "IT"-in-"market". Hence "complaints can be golden" to innovation activity.

Presuming complaints as fabricated or engineered; sporadic or rare can be ruinous to the enterprise itself leave alone the question of innovation activity. Likewise absence of customer complaints should not be mistaken as defect-free quality and irritant-free customer service. More often than not it means that customer has turned indifferent due to a sense of helplessness and/or despondency.

Therefore it is worthwhile to get the information on lapses in the quality and service directly from the customer in order to set appropriate targets of quality and service for the innovation project. Such an aggressive and positive approach should also bring forth valuable ideas for improving quality and service. Thus, seeking customer complaints, soliciting his views and ideas on improving quality and service do help to render the innovation task customer-driven; and thus enhances the chance of its success.

Quality and Cost

Cost is vital and important. Cost reduction through eliminating wastage, excess consumption, over time, rejection, substandard, rework has to be achieved in all functional areas. Cost reduction exercise should be carried out as a regular, normal, routine, consistent activity and not through "drives". These are healthy indisputable measures.

But in reality cost reduction exercise unintentionally takes a wrong direction as could be seen from the following common, typical, real experience. These can cause unintentional crippling blow to quality and even company's image.

- Fall in house-keeping standards
- Fall in standards of canteen
- Postponing maintenance jobs
- Process-changes without fully understanding their effect on quality .
- Eliminating distinctive and differenciating features of a product.
- Loss of product identity at consumer end; damage to "perceived quality".

Cost reduction should mean replacing luxury with austerity and not stifling creativity; relaxing quality levels; eliminating product features which consumers perceived as value and distinctiveness of the product. But the latter ones do invariably happen more often than not under the influence of cost reduction. Innovation activity aimed at cost reduction should be wary of achieving it through compromising on quality. In the long run such an approach proves to be counter productive if not disastrous. Innovation teams should not be enthusiastic in achieving cost reduction through cutting corners on quality in its wider sense. When it comes to quality and services affecting consumers, the emphasis must be on revenue enhancement through various measures. Use of the concept of "perceived quality" already mentioned is one such measure. Another one is based on the concept of "Earning-your-way-in" as against "Buying-your-way-in". Japan offers an illustration.

In the days when imperialistic power governed and controlled international trade, to gain entry into the market, Japan adopted "Buying-your-way-in" approach. It consisted of seeking market entry through low-cost with marginal-quality. After World War II with the lapse of imperialistic power when colonies gained freedom and sought economic emancipation, Japan changed the approach to "Earning-your-way-in". It consisted of market entry through high-quality with economic cost; retaining and expanding market-share through superior and exceptional quality and service to customer; and both being ably backed up by continuous innovation. Japan's present day economic status derived out of its supremacy in quality is world-recognised, a case of revenue enhancement approach.

"Buying-your-way-in" is a fall-out of cost-reduction thought-process. It is short-sighted. It is ever under the threat of competition from sources of better quality and competitive price. Innovation-activity in an enterprise gets stunted in this low-cost with marginal quality approach. "Earning-your-way-in" is linked to revenue enhancement. With this approach, innovation temper would be on top-gear and in a state of readiness to meet newer demands of quality and services.

Love of Product

Love is a powerful emotion. It establishes an emotional-bond; motivates and energises human endeavour to achieve better results; blossoms a shrivelled mind and a sunken heart; spurs action.

Such a powerful emotion must be built into ethos of work. Love in the context of quality-means "Love of product"; product meaning goods of the enterprises or the services offered by it or both."Love of Product" integrated with work achieves quality: sweeper sees the beauty and value of good-house-keeping and does the job with respect; like-wise despatch clerk pastes envelopes properly; worker gets his food served with a smile in canteen; loader handles cargo with care and caution; courteous clarification of accounts clerk convinces the irritated customer; defective piece gets discarded by assembly operator himself; field sales man shall be ever alert to keep consumer satisfied etc. In short, when love mingles with work quality gets reflected in the job of every one at grass root level.

Innovation activity and persons involved in it are no exception. In the context of innovation activity, it means an emotionally linked bond with the innovation project. This transforms itself, for instance in any project concerning product/process as one of acquiring thorough knowledge of the product; its touch, look, smell, feel, performance and anatomy; types of failures it suffers from and the several ways of its misuse/wrong use; the nature of charm it holds to customer as well as its seemingly simple things that hurt the customer etc. All these several things are minor individually. But collectively they are a formidable and valuable input to innovation activity that help develop new product/process/service to meet the needs of the market and achieve success in market place.

Conclusion

Quality systems and procedures are invariably followed in any innovation project right from design to despatch through all intermediary operations. To these need to be integrated the concepts briefly expounded in this chapter. This will orient the quality dimensions of the innovation project properly to the needs of the day and enhances the success of a project.

7

PROMOTING INNOVATION

Introduction

Earlier chapters have dealt with the need for innovation, meaning of innovation, peculiarities of innovation process, time-element in innovation activity and concepts of quality to be recognised therein. To achieve success in an innovation project, the several points covered in these chapters need to be assimilated and practised. These require an environment conducive to promote innovation in an enterprise.

Mere wishing to have such an environment does not help. It is necessary to build such an environment through concrete deeds and actions. Some of these are dealt with in this chapter.

Deeds and Actions

Deeds and actions related to building an environment congenial to promote innovation are as follows and they are briefly discussed hereunder :

- Ideas : encourage
- Failures : have a right attitude
- Informality and Simplicity : maintain
- Change : welcome
- Competence : keep-up
- "Hygiene and House-keeping" : keep away
- "Ownership" : develop

Ideas – Encourage

"Ideas rule the world". This is a familiar concept. There is no dispute about it. But in reality, attitudes and actions go counter to generate ideas. Hence the first and foremost requirement is to ensure that there is a positive thrust to encourage ideas in every functional area; implement the worthwhile ones to its logical end; review the implementation programme with the same spirit, concern, priority, and regularity as is done for production, sales revenue or profitability in the on-going business.

Some of the ground rules to be noted are as follows. They cover the positive ones that need to be practised and the negative ones to be avoided. The negative ones do crop-up unintentionally for the sole purpose of encouraging ideas ! This is paradoxical, but no doubt a reality.

- Ideas and insights are only raw materials. They are not finished products. An idea is like a baby. It is tender and fragile. Therefore, ideas need to be fostered through love and encouragement. By this they grow to reach their full potential.
- Ideas flow in plenty where they are not

  * Impaired by conventional habits, thinking and approach
  * Straightaway judged and evaluated by the same standards as applicable to the ones tried and proved.
  * Thwarted by responses like "what is new about the idea" "it is not practicable", "in what way it differs from the way it is being done now". In such an atmosphere no one comes out with any new ideas as the environment appears to be one of snubbing the originators of ideas.

- Congenial atmosphere to generate ideas are characterised by

  * existence of a positive attitude to listen to the ideas objectively;
  * aggresively looking for the merits of the idea
  * recognising the demerits with the purpose of rendering the idea more robust.

- As noted earlier, innovation process is synergy-dependent. Therefore, it is necessary to discuss the ideas with functional groups including potential customers who are essential to make a success of the ideas.
- Communicating rough ideas with all concerned ensures rapid,

effective innovation with certainty. Lone contributors have little or no chance of succeeding in the context of the present industrial and technological complexity.

– In the early stages of the creative phase it is desirable not to over plan and over formalize. Both discourage the development of ideas. On the other hand there must be a certain amount of free-wheeling freedom to visit other departments, customers and suppliers for exchange of information and to test assumptions.

– Do not always look upon ideas as original, sophisticated and capable of achieving breakthroughs. As already noted, simple, ordinary, common ones can turn out to be a great innovation success. Small changes in the product/process can bring in spectacular results.

– Provide resources and organisational support to the one who has come up with an idea provided it makes sense to him and willing to work on it. This helps to "fix the idea" involving its originator no matter to what level of organisational heirarchy he belongs to. Such a practice demonstrates that "ideas" are to be followed by "deeds" to make them worthwhile. It also gives a favourable twist to generation of ideas that it is an exercise not in "ivorytower thinking" or "blue sky dreaming" but in the "shop-floor".

– It is to be recognised that in the hard reality of the process of taking IT to market and achieving market impact, ideas originally considered as brilliant, fail; thought to be silly, succeed; hopeful ones as feasible, peters out. Therefore, at the start no judgemental label like brilliant, impractical, stupid should be attached to any ideas. Such an attitude kills the generation of ideas and their pursuit to the logical end.

Failure – Have a Right Attitude

"Failures are a stepping stone to success". It is an old adage. Its understanding and practice is crucial to innovation. As already noted, the very process of innovation is capricious, not straight and full of uncertainties. In such a field of activity failures are bound to occur and has to be tolerated. Such an understanding coupled with its practice reflect the organistional maturity in managing innovation.

Commonly these are understood and even spoken of elequently

by heads of organisation in learned seminars and conferences. But situation at "home", is that the one who encounters failure even in a good try gets the sack. This reflects credibility-gap. It gives a real jolt to innovation activity causing a serious set-back.

Ground rules on understanding of failure in innovation activity and handling of failures are as follows :

- Innovation means taking IT to market and achieving social/ economic impact. For this it is necessary that IT should be reliable and robust. Both these can be achieved through
  * generating failure data fast in a planned and deliberate manner.
  * failure data must be fairly extensive so as to catch all instances/types of failure that the process/product can encounter.
  * understanding the physics, chemistry and mechanics of each type of failure.
  * devising suitable corrective measures to prevent all the failures.
- The emphasis is on generating failure data which are of immense learning value for taking measures to develop a reliable robust product/process that can stay well in the market.
- Thus, failure is a sacred word in the context of innovation and is welcome as it helps to achieve success in the innovation project.
- Failure of a good try is limited success. Classical illustration of this concept is reflected in the reaction of Edison to his associates when they felt exasperated in not finding a suitable metal for filament even after screening scores of metals. Edison's reaction was that their efforts showed the ones unfit for filament making, a limited success.
- In innovation activity, failures are normal and even necessary. They have to be tolerated. Failures of good tries are to be even celebrated for their learning value. Therefore, individuals should not be held responsible for failures of good tries.
- Failure due to negligence, irresponsible action and hollow bravery have no place and must be avoided. Persons responsible for such failures must be held accountable.

There are always two forces – fear of failure and desire to achieve success. The above ground rules if practiced well, eliminate the fear of genuine failure and thus the energy level needed to achieve success gets doubled. The debilatative influence of the fear of failure gets mitigated.

Elimination of the fear of genuine failure has also its another beneficial fall-out. If a certain project were not to achieve the desired result even after a good deal of efforts, the absence of the fear of failure encourages the team to abandon the project and thus avoid waste of resources. The two types of situations – "near success", "continue, do not abandon; break-through is round the corner" – discussed earlier that are common in innovation activity can be avoided when there is no fear of failure. Therefore lack of fear of genuine failure promotes effective utilisation of the scarce resources of innovation.

Informality and Simplicity

Bureaucracy and heirarchy are the natural bottlenecks of innovation activity. They impede progress and generate frustration. Organisational structure, policies, systems and procedures that bureaucracy represents do have as their original intention to generate, sustain and improve growth-momentum of an enterprise. But over a period of time they turn out to be "a well of molasses"; one cannot get anything in or out; one cannot move-up or side-ways.

If bureaucracy is not watched, unchecked and not pruned it grows like a weed to sap the very life of the enterprise through untold delays, wastage of time and spreading gloom of frustration all round. This is no exaggeration. It could be seen, for instance in returning of purchase requisition by an assistant way down the level for want of an authorised signature in the requisition. Informality and simplicity in work set-up, and inter-personal relationship constitute a right-step in the direction of debureaucratisation. They must get reflected in day-to-day actions. Few of these mentioned hereunder are only indicative of such deeds and actions. They are not exhaustive.

- Oblivious to levels; free and open communication and contact. In the 60's it was a sight to see late Prof. JBS Haldane the renowned scientist in typical Indian dress mixing freely with his students and spending most of his time with them at Indian

> Statistical Institute, Calcutta. Junior most research assistant had no hesitation in knocking his door at any time. Similar was the case with the late Prof. S. R. Ranganathan the doyen of library science when his brain-child DRTC (Documentation Research and Training Centre) was born at Bangalore. All his students used to be with him during his morning walk discussing research projects.

As against these examples, the commonly found pattern can be termed as "coconut model : can't be reached while on the tree as it is too tall to reach; and also while on the ground as its shell is too hard to reach the kernel.

This model is reinforced by equally rigid practices like "communicate through proper channel", "put proposals to work after taking appropriate clearance", etc. These inhibit and cripple innovation activity.

There must be a free flow information and contact at all levels of management relevant to an innovation project. Thus for example, if MD of an organisation is accessible easily for consultation/approvals on an innovation project, it sets an example of easy accessibility to others down the line and helps to break the heirarchical rigidities in the matter of contact and communication. During the discussions, there must be respect for the idea and its originators no matter what their levels are; discussions must be centred round on strengthening the idea through use of authority. Such a practice does help to debureaucratise the environment and help progress of innovation project.

The out-put of the innovation team must be exposed to a wider section from time to time to invite interaction on a broader and larger scale. This practice helps to break the departmental barriers.

Simplicity, informality, non-bureaucratic set-up must be transparent and also manifest through concrete evidence. Thus for example, furniture and fittings, must be more functional and not luxurious. As far as the innovation team is concerned the differences in the levels of persons within the team should not get reflected in any way through the type of furniture, fixtures, curtains, etc. which are invariably used by the heirarchy to reflect the status.

Place of eating though neat, clean, well-lighted, calm and quiet, it should not be compartmentalised to reflect the levels. Transport, library facilities are also to be made available to innovation team at all odd times to suit their needs. Sponsoring of candidates to appropriate seminars/conferences should be need-based and not heirarchy-dependent. These are some of the common deeds to bring about an atmosphere of informality and simplicity.

Providing just the adequate or even marginally less staff and funds is also a means to ensure that innovation team remains ever alert on the effective use of resources and avoid laxity.

Change – Welcome

Innovation means change. Everyone agrees that there must be continuous change for the better. But reality is totally different. It is one of offering maximum resistance to change. The reasons for this are not far to seek. Change evokes different kinds of reactions in different personnel but all rallying round the same common point : maintain *status quo*. Change means threat, fear, strain to adopt to the new, stress of acquiring different knowledge and skills, nuisance and interference etc. Therefore, in general, a negative and even hostile attitude prevail towards change. Even in a mature organistion, a passive and "what-can't-be-cured-must-be-endured" type of apathetic attitude prevails.

Yet another common reason to fight change is related to the manner in which functional/divisional managers at the top operate. They seldom function together. Rarely do they bring to bear on any innovation project their collective intelligence and experience. They do not function as "elder and wiser heads" by reshaping the idea to make it more workable. In effect they do not take the role of prime movers of change. Instead they take up the evaluative and judgemental role. This evaluative attitude instead of supporting role acts as a drag in bringing about changes for the better. This results in generating more of resistance to change. The evaluative role is perceived by the rest as a non supportive role for the proposed changes. The outcome is that the same pattern flows down the line. Consequence of this is victory of "status-quo" over "change". The above typical situation has to be transformed whereby an enterprise welcomes change, sheds fear of change, masters change and evokes change. Some of the ground rules that facilitate an enterprise to have a pro-change environment are as follows:

– Honour the "Champions", the ones who bringforth ideas,

implement them and achieve tangible results. In the beginning this can cover the cases where the results achieved may be of significance only within the company with no market impact. Champion must be honoured "then & there" without delay.

- The one who walks falters and gets the scar. Scars-difficulties encountered, mess-up caused-are symbols of a performer. Success in bringing about a change cannot be without scars. Any performer cannot be without scars. Promote performers with "scars". It is a positive recognition of those who successfully implement change programmes to achieve better results.
- Take note of all instances where traditions are broken constructively to enhance performance without any embarrassment to the enterprise. Make these instances widely known; Celebrate the significant ones.
- Performers with scars must be encouraged to speak out the failures encountered before achieving success. Common tendency is to cover-up, be silent on failures or attribute success to "flash of genius". These should be avoided. One being outspoken on failures encountered before achieving success helps to fight the fear of failure and builds courage in people to promote, accept and succeed in change programmes.
- Do disturb routine operations for development work. By this, importance attached by the management to innovation activity is adequately demonstrated.
- "Change" needs leaders, the ones who are capable of communicating their visions of change to the rest in the enterprise, sell the change, shape it and adopt it. Identify such shapers of change and entrust them with the task of introducing change. In effect they are leaders of innovation projects in the enterprise. Without such leaders with courage of conviction and commitment besides being good at communication, ideas will disappear and evaporate; the bureaucratic set-up which has already conditioned people to adhere and maintain *status quo* would perpetuate.
- Top functional managers must frequently wander the work place, mix freely with persons engaged in "change" activities, share their visions, contribute to their enhancement and support their activities.
- Adopt the healthy organisational practice of shifting the successful senior managers now in-charge of big and profitable

on-going-business to look after the small but future oriented jobs. This brings about an environment that welcomes change, seeks change and adopts change.

Competence – Keep Up

Everyone agrees about the need and importance of competence in the context of innovation activity. Few realise the characteristic features of competence; fewer still, the know-how to keep-up competence. To be competent, is largely a matter for individuals concerned. Enterprise can do certain things to enhance one's competence. But it is precious little compared to self-drive and self-urge to be competent.

The characteristic features of competence are as follows :

- Competence is transitory and not permanent. Executives generally speak more of their yesterday's conquests and achievements; but very little of the present and almost nothing of the plans of tommorrow. This reflects the transient nature of competence although not realised to be so.
- Certificate of competence has a short-shelf-life and needs to be updated constantly. A person found competent yesterday need not necessarily be so to-day. It is like hair on the head, never there to stay all the time. Speaking of yesterdays glory and conquests is indicative of the degenerating level of competence.
- Competence is largely a matter of not what one thinks about himself. But it is an issue that has to be demonstrated; demonstrated almost continuously-not a flash in the pan. It is not enough for the individual to feel that he is competent; it is for the others- superiors, peers, juniors – to perceive that the individual is competent. In cricket, one gets an acclaim as a good batsman or bowler on the basis of his on-going performance and not how he performed in the last series. Same thing is true for any field activity to be judged as competent.
- Competence can be acquired. One can learn to be competent.
- The nature of competence changes from level to level of the organisational heirarchy. At the grass root level, competence relates to thorough job-knowledge, ability to overcome quality and production problems. At the level of divisional head, competence is reflected in his ability to adopt new methods and

approaches to improve productivity, quality, safety; identify new areas of application of the product and aggressively enter new markets; sail well with management as well as other functional groups to ensure the best of their help, support and co-operation are always available.

Few of the methods for acquiring and enhancing competence are as follows :

- There must be learning zeal in individuals to acquire new skills, knowledge and eagerness to take-up new assignments and cease new opportunities/area of work.
- Enterprise must also create a learning atmosphere. Sponsoring of competent personnel to technical exhibition, professional seminars/conference can be one such way.
- Self-introspection and assessment at regular intervals of time on the new skills acquired, new jobs undertaken, new responsibilities discharged etc. can be of great value to an individual; it motivates one to be competent.
- Make it obligatory for the senior management staff to submit self-assessment-report on their own performance. The dominant position in such a report needs to be given to new ideas initiated and implemented during the report-period; results achieved in the category "new and different" as well as "better and more". Pay hike should be linked to one's contribution to innovation efforts.

Hygiene and House-keeping – Keep Away

The jobs related to "Hygiene and house-keeping" are those that are neither result producing nor professional. But they are necessary and important jobs. Jobs of this category at times, get entrusted to those meant to be utilised for innovation activity. By this, their time and focus get diverted on activities not strictly theirs. Such a waste of resources must be avoided.

Typical examples of activities that can be considered as "Hygiene and House-keeping" jobs for innovation personnel are :

- maintenance/upkeep of sophisticated equipments and instruments

- Trouble shooting assignments which could best be handled by shop personnel
- accident investigations
- serving on personnel selection, departmental promotion committees
- Invitation to participate in meetings which they need not necessarily attend to.

Ownership – Develop

Success of an innovation activity rests on the innovation teams's high level of commitment and dedication; perseverance and energy. The team must be obsessed with the success of the project. It must have a religious – fervour to pursue the project perfectly to the point of its success. Such a situation can be established by bringing the concept of the team being the "owner" of the project.

Therefore, the concept of "ownership" must be institutionalised. One way is to set-up self-contained, self-sustainable autonomous (on a time bound basis) product divisions totally responsible for technology, products, process, market development, production, finance including long term compensation plan.

Associating the names of individuals in patents to be taken, is now a poor incentive for innovation. Reason for this is that many patents are still in the "sterile, dust free, pristine, temperature-controlled laboratories" with no hope of seeing the light of the day.

Enterprise should develop necessary vision and nerve to set-up autonomous units with ease. It transforms innovation as a business. In fact "innovation is business".

Innovation without business-sense and business-base remains only "inner urge", "grand curiosity", dream, fashion and "green-house at great cost".

Conclusion

What soil conditions are to seeds to produce a good crop, a congenial environment of an enterprise is to innovation for achieving success. No idea gets generated must less blossom to achieve market impact. Hence, it is very important to promote a congenial environment where ideas comeforth freely; they pass through creative phase; the worthwhile ones are taken up as innovation projects and market success is achieved.

Deliberate and planned deeds and actions are necessary to create such a congenial environment for innovation activity as a whole. The various deeds and actions briefly discussed in this chapter can go a long way in building a favourable, congenial environment in an enterprise for it to succeed well with its innovation projects.

8

ORGANISING FOR INNOVATION

Background

The earlier chapters have dealt with different aspects of innovation activity right from its meaning to deeds and actions that are required to promote innovation activities in an enterprise through a clear understanding of the factors affecting time-dimension in innovation activity; the quality concepts relevant to the activity.

It has also been noted that innovation is a key-result area and therefore the competence of top management would be judged by its performance in the field of managing innovation. All these reflect the importance of organising for innovation on a sound basis.

Formidable Task

No industrial enterprise is new to the task of innovation although it may not have known all its intricacies and peculiarities besides recognising its overriding importance and the priority it has to have in the managerial functions of the present day.

Many enterprises have also organised for innovation. A typical picture of the way innovation is being carried out at present is summarised in Exhibit 8.1. A perusal of this indicates that at present, innovation activity:

- is centred around only R&D department and not organised as a company-wide activity;
- is very much hampered by bureaucractic systems and procedures;
- is carried out more as a hobby than as a committed exercise;
- is handicaped by lack of proper managerial help and support;
- is there, more as a fashion to project the enterprise as being modern and up to date.

Thus the practice of innovation is far from satisfactory both in its intent and content. Stupendous effort is called for to organise innovation on a sound basis. This chapter outlines a suitable approach to organise innovation.

Organising for Innovation: An Approach

For any activity to yield its expected results it has to be properly organised. This exercise in general requires a clear understanding of the activity; its peculiarities, adoption of strategies that suit the activity to achieve the set goals; means of assessing/evaluating the results from time to time; organisational mechanism to monitor the progress and take corrective measures at the earliest as and when needed.

This general approach holds good for innovation activity also and it can be stipulated as hereunder:

(a) Correct understanding of what innovation is and the manner in which it is different from improvement, invention or discovery.
(b) Creating an environment that promotes innovation.
(c) Obsession with customers; customers' service and such an obsession enveloping the enterprise as a whole and innovation activity in particular.
(d) Adoption of right innovation strategy.
(e) Promoting innovation through "sponsors" and "team work" as "half-way-house" measure; and establishing autonomous and separate units.
(f) Evaluation and monitoring.
(g) Resorting to certain healthy organisational practices.

Each one of the steps mentioned above is briefly dealt with.

Understanding of Innovation

The term 'Innovation' is confusing. It means different things to different persons. Innovation is not a technical term. It is not necessarily linked with science and technology. Innovation is not mere improvement. Innovation is not just discovery or invention. Innovation is an economic/social term. Innovation is the task of taking an 'IT' — product/process/service — to market and achieving market impact. Innovation is an activity carried out within an enterprise to achieve an external impact, in 'market'. Therefore, innovation has to be customer-driven and market-oriented.

All these several attributes of innovation have already been discussed in the earlier chapters 'Innovation-meaning' and 'Understanding of innovation process'. What innovation is not, has also been highlighted.

These need to be recognised by top management to have a unified understanding. This is a prerequisite while organising for innovation.

The following characteristics of the innovation process discussed in the chapter "Understanding of Innovation Process" need to be kept in view and taken note of while organising for innovation:

Basics not to be lost sight of are:

- Recognise innovation is "IT" in 'market' and avoid the attitude of 'IT' - vs - 'Market'.
- 'Near success' is not success.
- Don't carry out the project beyond a reasonable time limit under the mistaken notion that success is round the corner;
- Ideas selected after thorough scrutiny and screening, do not imply their success.

Ensure the following :

- cast the net wide – more experiments and trials;
- know well the 'failure' in its entirety as applicable to the project;
- free flow of ideas from diverse sources
- bringing to bear the right synergy on the project.

Creating an Environment for Promoting Innovation

Having an environment of the right type is fundamental to achieve success in an innovation activity. There are specific actions to be taken and deeds to be performed in an enterprise for building a congenial environment. These deeds and actions are as follows:

- Ideas – encourage
- Failures – have a right attitude and celebrate/tolerate genuine failures.

- Informality and simplicity – maintain.
- Change – welcome.
- Competence – keep up.
- 'Hygiene and house keeping' – keep away
- 'Ownership' – develop.

Each of the above has been dealt with in Chapter 4. These need to be put into action for building an environment that promotes innovation.

The task of building the congenial environment lies not in the circulars and notes circulated by top management but in its correct and consistent actions and deeds. The governing principle is 'walk the talk' on each deed and action enumerated above.

Obsession with Customers and Customer Service

The success of innovation lies in achieving its impact on customers. Therefore, obsession with customers, their needs, their changing preferences, the service rendered to them at all points of contact including the often neglected areas like telephone courtesy, billing, packing and forwarding etc. must be manifest in the enterprise as a whole. It helps innovation activity.

Measures to be taken to develop an obsession with customers and their needs enumerated here under have been discussed in the chapters 'Innovation and Quality' and 'Time-element in innovation activity'. These are to be meticulously adopted in the enterprise:

- Recognise Quality as a broad-based concept comprising of: reliability and safety over the entire life of the product; and elements of 'perceived quality'
- Recognise that mere conformance to the set national/ international quality standards is only a measure of minimum quality capability of an enterprise and reflects mediocre performance; aim at quality leadership.
- Prefer revenue enhancement approach to quality.
- Do not ignore complaints of customer; 'complaints can be golden'
- Develop in the enteprise as a whole positive 'love of product'; product representing the goods and services of the company.
- Prefer 'good' for 'perfect'.

– Link innovation projects with lead users/suppliers
– Give the pride of place to 'non-innovation' personnel in the innovation activities.

Adoption of Right Type of Innovation Strategy

Innovation is not an unstructured work. Innovation is not an arena for a free-lance poet. It is very much a systematic work. It is also strategy based. Development of this outlook on innovation is largely due to the contributions of management philosopher-thinker-practitioner Peter Drucker. He has expounded his thoughts, ideas and practical guidelines in his book 'Innovation and Entreprenuership'.

It has been pointed out that majority of successful innovations are the outcome of having exploited 'change'. Therefore, systematic innovation comprises of:

– Identifying sources of change
– Examining change in each source
– Continuously monitoring changes noticed/anticipated
– Utilising the changes as innovative opportunity to accomplish something "new and different".

'Changes' have also been classified into different categories for ease of identification and understanding. This classification propounded by Drucker is as follows:

Within the enterprise:

– Unexpected success/failure/outside event.
– Incongruity between reality as it actually is and as it 'ought to be' or as it is assumed to be
– Innovation based on process need
– Changes in industry structure or market structure

Outside the enterprise:

– Demographics (population changes)
– Changes in perception
– New knowledge, scientific and non-scientific

It is to be noted that these sources do overlap with one another. But each one has its own distinct characteristics; is amenable to separate analysis; is inherently as important/productive as any other source; is arranged in descending order of reliability and predictability.

For an enterprise at a given point of time not all but only a few of the sources of change may be relevant; it is necessary to recognise the relevant ones and accordingly shape the innovation activities. This reemphasises the point that every enterprise must have a means to scan the environment to know the changes that are taking place and use the information to fashion its innovation activities.

After having recognised the innovation opportunity the next step is one of choosing the strategy that suits the opportunity. On the subject of strategy also, the general approach expounded by Peter Drucker is of immense value and use. For purpose of clear understanding, he categorises the strategies as hereunder:

- Strategy of leadership.
- Creative limitation.
- Entrepreneurial judo
- Finding and occupying a specialised 'ecological niche'
- Changing the economic characteristics of a product, a market or industry.

These strategies are not mutually exclusive. There is overlapping and cannot always be sharply differentiated. But each has its own prerequisites to be satisfied, limitations to be noted and risks to be recognised. Apart from these differentiations, each strategy requires a certain type of specific discipline on the part of the one opting for it. Each of these strategies has been excellently dealt with and illustrated by many examples in the book already referred to.

For a chosen innovation project, the type of strategy that closely fits it has to be adopted and appropriate course of actions need to be taken.

Sponsors', 'Team-work', Autonomous and Separate Units

Innovation projects are like infants – puny, delicate and struggling to exist. They need to be tended and taken care of like infants. Any innovation idea requires extraordinary amount of work as it is new. It also involves many things to learn; encounters many mistakes and false starts. These are inevitable. To comprehend and cope up with these, wholetime attention is needed.

Generally, overall responsibility for innovation projects are delegated to the ones who are in-charge of the 'big and profitable' lines of business, an 'adult'. This implies that innovation project is assigned as a part-time responsibility. This very approach denies an innovation project the attention it needs and priority it deserves. Attention and priority are always the prerogative of the 'big and profitable'. The result is innovation projects die of neglect. Thus a sure way to choke innovation activities is to tie them up with an ongoing business.

There is yet another way of thwarting innovation. It is to say "NO" to every new idea and keep-on saying it for a year or two. It is enough. No one comes up with any new idea.

Enteprises must guard against these two approaches that sound the death knell of innovation quietly, quickly and surely. One way to safeguard the innovation projects is to have a person fairly high-up in the heirarchy known for his success in the tasks of taking 'IT to market', exclusively in-charge of innovation projects. He is generally referred to as 'Sponsor'. He must have the capacity to understand the problems of innovation projects; has full time at his disposal for understanding the problems and dynamism to overcome the difficulties. He acts as a protector of the project when it falters; wards-off bureaucratic interference; helps the projects to gain access to resources, information, specialised support, if any. He has faith in the project and sufficient patience to support it. He has the wisdom to distinguish between temporary set-back and terminal-problem; and if latter were to be the case, has the courage of conviction to terminate the project.

The top management must also have its confidence in the sponsor that he always has the interest of the Company while providing his protection, support and counsel to projects. Thus, by design an enterprise can ensure the progress of innovation projects through the concept of 'sponsor'. Otherwise the risk of innovation projects facing fast unnoticed premature extinction is very high.

Team Work

The nature of innovation activity in the present context is not the work of a single person or single department. No one functional area can be responsible for taking "IT to market" and achieving market impact. If an innovation project were to be promoted as a departmental activity, implementation gets bogged down due to lack of understanding or support from other departments. Therefore, it is necessary to form a multidisciplinary team which 'owns' the project. Members of the team need to be drawn from marketing, manufacturing, R&D, Design etc. so that each one contributes his specialised knowledge to the success of the project.

It is desirable to bring into the team the ones who exhibit the different traits of a champion. In fact all the traits of a champion cannot be found in the same person to the same degree. But a team of 'champions' can bring to bear on the project the impact of the total champion-spirit and ensure its success. This is the positive justification for having team approach to innovation activity.

As already mentioned, the members of the team are assigned to work on the project on whole time basis and not part time; no member works in an advisory capacity; and the team leader is a doer and not a dreamer.

The team approach brings the benefit interfunctional integration to innovation activity. The outcome of the team work is primarily establishing the total feasibility of the project including market success.

Autonomous Units

Once the feasibility is established, the stage is set for commercial operation. No general rule can be specified for scaling up. It depends on each case. But when a project reaches commercialisation, it should be established as a separate autonomous unit which has to stand on its own performance within the set time limit. This practice ensures success of the project; motivates well the people involved in an innovation project; provides appropriate growth opportunities; promotes intrepreneurship.

The Bhabha Atomic Research Centre (BARC) serves as an excellent example of spinning off of several enterprises. The various divisions of the present Electronics Corporation of India Ltd. (ECIL), were at one time several departments of BARC. When they reached 'critical-mass' they were spun-off as separate business enterprises under ECIL.

As a successful product/service is developed, it should be

spun-off as a separate self-sustaining enterprise. It helps the new venture to grow fast. This philosophy in 3-M of America is termed as "Divide and Grow". This process provides powerful motivation for continuous innovation; compels people to seek and identify new business opportunity as an on-going activity.

For divisional heads of on-going, 'big and profitable' lines, it should be made compulsory that they should sponsor and support a new product/process/service which can eventually grow into a separate enterprise. It should be made clear to the divisional heads that it is not enough to keep-up the bottom-line performance of their division but they should also show their ability to spin-off as many new ventures as possible.

The ease with which an enterprise spins-off a separate autonomous unit, reflects its competence as an innovative enterprise and it is an index of efficient management of innovation in the enterprise.

Evaluation and Monitoring

The evaluation and monitoring must primarily focus on the two parameters – results and time frame.

Regarding results, the comparison to be made is between results expected *vs* actual achievement as on the date of review. The same is applicable to time also. The pattern of review on results and time are given in below.

The frame work given is an over-simplified version. In reality review and monitoring is a painstaking exercise. The main thurst is to curb the tendencies to over-estimate or under-estimate results, the needs of time and other resources. More importantly the review should always aim at finding out (a) the resources — crunch and provide the same in time to ensure satisfactory progress (b) the gaps if any in 'knowledge' and 'know-how' ; and the means of filling up the gaps.

Care must be taken to curb the tendency to "show progress" during the review session when in fact there is no real tangible progress. Review session should also be used to identify in advance the projects likely to face terminal problems.

(a) Results.

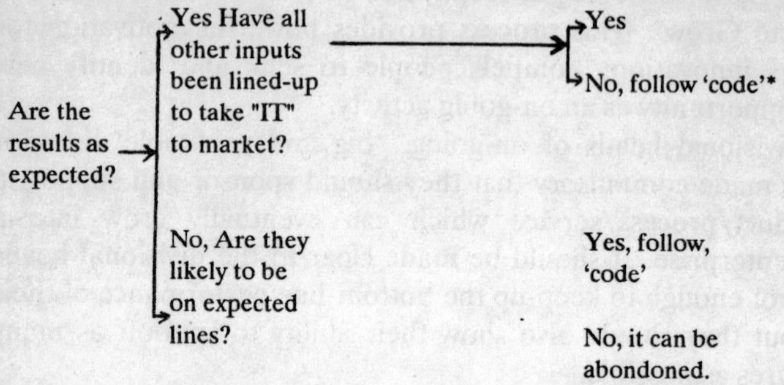

(b) Time

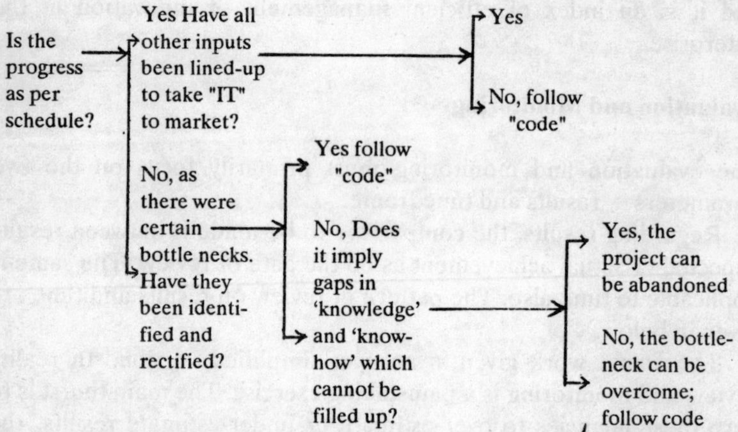

* Enumerate the action plan; take necessary action; set the revised schedule, covering even marketing efforts.

Certain Healthy Organisational Practices

Any enterprise can be innovative provided it strives to become innovative; puts adequate effort to learn the art of being innovative and also conform to the discipline that innovation demands. The last one essentially relates to organisational practices. Some of these which have greater relevance to innovation activities are as follows:

The work culture in the enterprise must reflect that the task of building an innovative enterprise and achieving success in an innovation project are largely a matter of smart and hard work that is focussed and purposeful; diligent, persistent and committed. It is also to be noted that if this type of work is lacking, no amount of knowledge, brilliance, intuition, ingenuity or talent would help to build an innovative enterprise and achieve success in innovation projects.

There must be the practice of reviewing at regular intervals of time every activity including products, process, systems and procedures to slough off of the ones that are worn out, obsolete or no longer productive. This exercise must also aim at identifying the mistakes, past failures, misdirected efforts of the past to avoid similar things from happening in the future. Such a simple exercise in tangible terms makes everyone future conscious and not gloat over the past success or lament over past lapses.

In every enterprise there would be individuals and sections who perform better than the rest. It is necessary to identify their distinguishing features: reasons for their success; the specific things they do which rest do not; the ones they are not doing but others do. These distinguishing features need to be made common to the enterprise as a whole.

To keep the corpse from not stinking is a heroic but futile job. It is common in many an enterprise that some of its best people are engaged in heroic but futile jobs. This is a waste of human resources. Therefore, there must be the healthy practice of freeing the performers to innovation work.

There must be a close vigilance on the innovation efforts of competitors – their areas of work, record of performance as an innovator, budget allotted etc.

Frequent interaction must be there between innovation teams and top management. The focal point of the interaction must be issues like areas of work to be taken up; type of contribution to be achieved in next two years; recognising areas of achievement that really makes a difference for the better in the performance of the enterprise, opportunities to be exploited etc.

Always purposeful action cannot be based only on data, analysis and market predictions. The importance of developments in the periphery can be missed by quantification exercise but not so when matched by sound judgement and intuition. Going by the market predictions, computer and aeroplane for instance would never have been a commercially successful ventures that they are now as the estimate for computers was only a dozen when it was developed in 1940 and aeroplane was never thought to be of any use in warfare. These are only a few of the many examples that highlight the importance to be given to sound judgement and intuition in decision making specially on innovation projects.

Any innovation project has to have a strong conceptual and perceptual base. It helps to have necessary insight to work on the project. Correct perception has to be acquired through actual deeds – go, see, feel, experience, touch, smell, look. Perceptions help to develop right concepts. Together they strengthen innovation activity.

The end result of the innovation work must evoke the question "This is obvious, why did I not think of it? It is the hall mark of simplicity. Simple things succeed well. Hence for the innovation to be effective and succeed in market place, its outcome should be simple and capable of being handled by ordinary persons.

The starting point of innovation must be as a rule modest small start, few people, small and limited market, little investment. This strategy helps to correct; make adjustments or effect quick changes as and when needed and thus ensure success of innovation. It also ensures focussed attention, yet another important factor contributing to success of innovation. Better to avoid the grandiose thought of 'Revolutionising the industry'.

The outcome of innovation must be of immediate applicability. Present and not future must be the concern of the innovation project. The success of innovation is determined by market impact. This implies that innovation must have its aim as achieving leadership and not necessarily spinning off a 'big business'. Aiming at leadership may bring in its train big business but not the other way round.

An Observation

From the above discussions it can be seen that the approach to organising for innovation is inherently different from the traditional heirarchical approach based on organisation-chart, who-reports-to whom, organisational-levels, departmentalisation, compatability of levels, span of control etc. which can be elegantly represented in paper.

The approach discussed is an organic net-work organisation that cannot be reduced to elegant presentation on paper. It cuts across organisational boundaries to bring about a greater degree of synergy;

takes suitable measures to build a congenial environment favouring growth of innovation; provides for a sponsor fairly high in the heirarchy facilitating timely flow of resources for innovation project and also protecting it from the ravaging effects of bureaucratic set-up; ensures spinning off of the project as a separate autonomous unit to eventually develop into a new separate self-sustaining product/service division.

It is far easier to guide and control a large work force engaged in routine standardized activities. The set procedures, systems, precedents and practices serve well the task of governance. Similar approach cripples innovation activity, demotivates creative people and in the end they either leave the organisation or stay as ornamental fixtures but disgruntled, disgusted and demoralised. The key thoughts and actions that earn loyalty, commitment, dedication and sense of accountability of the creative people are essentially freedom-for-action and resources-to-work. These aspects have been amply taken due care of in the approach to organising for innovation out lined above.

'Product/process liability' is assuming greater significance. Law suits for injuries caused by product/process can spell disaster to an enterprise including its closure. Liability laws have been enacted in a number of countries. Move is also set afoot towards personal liability of the engineers and technologists for product failures. Against this background, an enterprise must provide adequate freedom to develop a fool-proof 'IT' that is safe even in its wrongful usage. In practice, achieving this goal calls for intellectual/technological integrity on the part of innovation personnel by not taking short-cuts to please the top. Enterprise must also have an environment which does not encourage unhealthy short-cuts and compromises. In such an atmosphere, innovation activity flourishes well. Generally creative personnel look for enterprises whose remuneration packages may not necessarily be attractive but do offer work opportunities and environment wherein their creative ability can grow unfettered; technological independence is encouraged, respected and not required to be compromised with; and contributions made are honestly recognised in a fitting manner. All these needs have also been recognised and provided for in the organisational aspects of innovation discussed earlier.

Implementation

The first essential step in organising for innovation, is to conduct a programme titled "Managing Innovation – concepts and tasks" to all the key-personnel of an enterprise including its top management. The various topics covered in this book can in fact form the subject matter of the course.

To make the programme focused and relevant to the organisation, the current status of innovation in the enterprise must also be assessed and utilised in the programme. To accomplish this task, prior to the conduct of the programme an evaluation must be made of the perception the key persons-top and middle management – of the enterprise have on the current status of innovation activities in the enterprise as well as on its innovative environment. Such an evaluation can be made on the basis of the responses obtained to the questionnaires given in Exhibits 8.3 and 8.4. The programme can be spread over 4 days at a stretch lasting for about 5-6 hr, a day. This programme helps to:

(a) Unify the varying views and ideas of different functional groups on innovation.
(b) Dispel the prevailing wrong concepts on practice of innovation.
(c) Highlight the short-comings of the existing organisational set-up for carrying out innovation projects.
(d) Lay bare the deficiencies in the existing approach to and practice of innovation.
(e) Expose the recurrent problems facing innovation activities and
(f) Create an environment to accept changes to promote innovation on right lines.

There must be a follow-up action to consolidate the gains of the course. Follow up lies in taking a few simple innovation projects each having its own team and sponsors. The projects chosen must be fairly simple and capable of striking oil in market place. The main intention is that they should serve as simple working models to gain on-line experience in organising for innovation and put into practice the concepts and tasks relevant to the practice of innovation. A few quick successes will pave the way to achieve large scale results.

It should be recognised that transforming an existing enterprise into an innovative one means a total change in out look and attitude;

in short, administering a cultural shock. The approach to implementation outlined above brings out the desired cultural change smoothly with understanding and involvement, so essential to make the transformation into an innovative enterprise permanent.

Conclusion

We are in 'turbulent times' . This is a testing time for every institution. How well an institution is going to survive depends on its continued relevance to the needs of the day. History is replete with numerous examples of professions and institutions which have whithered away on account of their inability to brace themselves to weather ably the changing times and adapt themselves to the changing needs. This general phenomenon is equally true of industrial enterprises.

The only way an industrial enterprise can survive well is to be highly innovative. Any enterprise can be innovative provided it strives to become one. The various concepts, ideas and thoughts out-lined in this chapter can aid an industrial enterprise to organise itself as an innovative enterprise and thus ensure its survival that is socially meaningful and economically-healthy.

EXHIBIT 8.1

Typical Situation : Innovation Activity in an Enterprise

1. There is lack of understanding of 'what innovation is'. Innovation is mistaken as improvement. Innovation as a process of creating a "new and different", making the 'present' obsolete is not fully realised much less practised.
2. Innovation as a corporate function is not recognised and given its due priority.
3. Innovation activity revolves round 'R&D' department and therefore it holds the key for all innovation activities. Hence innovation activity is pursued only as a departmental activity – a narrow and isolated function; and not as a companywide activity whereby every department is innovation conscious and undertakes innovative work as applicable to it.
4. As innovation is a departmental activity, it ceases to be a multi-disciplinary, cross-functional activity to ensure fast success.
5. There is proliferation of job-classification and fine distinction between persons essentially concerned with the same type of job like senior operator, junior operator. This breads the familiar excuse 'This is not my job' and thus inhibits creative activity.
6. Bureaucracy hampers creative work. Too many steps and hurdles are involved in obtaining approvals and support for altering existing approaches or adopting new ones. This is frustrating for innovation work.
7. The atmosphere in the enterprise is one where fear of failure looms large for any one to take even simple ordinary genuine risk to try something new and different. There is the environment-induced-compulsion to play-safe and as per the 'book'. This kills initiative and effectively plugs the flow of ideas. Thus initiative and ideas the very foundation of innovation activity stands nicely demolished.
8. 'Technical hubris' – an organisational disease that treats technology as sacro sant and more important than customer and his needs which in fact the technology has to serve, blinds the

organisation to changes in market place.

Note

This blindness can reach a collosal scale to threaten the very existence of the unit. It is well described in the words attributed to an American Admiral 'that thing (atombomb) will never go off and I speak as an expert on explosives' when in fact the 'thing' was getting ready to go-off. Similarly key-persons of an enterprise suffering from technical hubris can inflict irreversible harm to their enterprise by lulling it with thoughts like 'change does not affect us', 'these changes are only momentary aberrations, it will go away' when in fact the changes are in the process of cutting-off of the market for the enterprise.

Sickness in cotton industry: two wheeler companies which were prosperous a few years ago but sick now; declining performance of cigarette industry abroad; photo-film industry based on acetate process being in jitters etc. are all examples of sickness arising out of having ignored the significance of 'changes'.

9. Excessive devotion to technology at the expense of the needs of customers and their changing preference has directed innovation efforts to perfecting technology and not to meet market needs. That is innovation efforts are not customer oriented and market driven. The result is disappointing results.
10. Existing organisational structure based on departmentalisation can suit the on-going business but not jobs related to innovation. The existing set-up renders any innovation job disconnected, disjointed and totally ineffective. The common experience of R&D giving the know-how of a new product to process development; process development to manufacturing; manufacturing to sales; sales finally reporting its unsuitability to market and each department in turn finding fault with the other that it did not get the right stuff without any concern for achieving success in the launching of the new product is the direct result of departmentalised structure. Here the name of the game is to defend departmental interests ignoring those of the company.
11. The management is not pragmatic and positive in its approach to innovation. Thus for example, it does not specify or help to evolve realistic parameters for an innovation project. If it does, it is one

of an impractical type like developing an 'IT' that has little or no risk of market failure; yielding better returns than the existing one; requiring little or no change in production set-up; involving little or no investment; and completing the task in a very short time. The net result is that no innovation project gets cleared when scrutinised against these criteria.

12. The top management represented by Divisional Heads do not function like promoters of innovation. They do not collectively bring to bear their wisdom and experience to strengthen the innovation projects and help them to progress fast. On the other hand, they take up the evaluative and judgemental role that dampens the initiative and retards the progress.
13. The dominant emphasis in all activities going under the name of innovation and/or development are all essentially cost reduction programmes; not even cost-effective ones. The outcome is the casuality of ideas that call for investment first to achieve a better revenue later.
14. Enterprises doing extremely well become complacent and turn indifferent to innovation under the mistaken notion that their bottom-line performance will continue to remain high as at present.
15. Enterprise not taking up innovation activity as a serious function due to wrong bias that there is not much point in bringing about improvements/changes when competitors have done nothing.
16. Enterprises getting grounded due to market shrinkage inspite of the products being good and competitive in quality and price. The reasons for this is due to the enterprise refusing to take notice of the changes in market place by being very much internally focussed to the neglect of changes in the market. Examples of this are plenty: valve radio by transistors, liquid-ink-pens being replaced by ball point pens, buttons by zip, slide-rule by electronic calculator, glassware by plastics etc. In each of these cases there was nothing lacking quality and price-wise in the products that were replaced. But they were edged out of market because customers preferred the alternative ones.
17. Professional prejudices and cynicism dominate dampening innovation activities. Cynicism has its own charming way of existing in an enterprise. This is best illustrated by the reaction of cynics on the banks of the river Hudson on the eve of the launching of the steam boat; at the start, remark was 'steam

would never move a heavy object' and when the boat started moving the remark was 'They will never be able to stop it'.

18. The well established base of the product – high customer favour, heavy investment in existing manufacturing operations, agreement on production and productivity with unions, statutory clearances already obtained – would get affected by any changes. This situation by itself is used not to adopt any change for the better and the top – management is a mute supporter of the *status quo*. It is to this attitude that sickness of the many Iron and Steel works, Paper mills in the country can be attributed to. Likewise the prosperity of many of the old establishments in this field like Tata Steel is attributed to not having fallen a victim of maintaining the status-quo on the grounds it cannot be altered.
19. When something new is being tried, the number of road blocks put on the way turn out to be infinite and the change-efforts suffer a set back. The common, simple, silent, unnoticeable but effective road-block used to stall a change proposal is that of the departmental head simply sitting over it without responding to it for a while.
20. The concern for innovation as judged from top management is only skin-deep and not backed by deeper convictions. This is reflected in centralised control of innovation activity; directing the activity as per the chosen path without examining all other alternatives or options, the chosen path being held as a close preserve shrouded with secrecy.
21. Innovation is treated more as a hobby. It is delegated to the same persons saddled with routine responsibilities of the big and profitable on-going products. Hence it is taken up whenever the 'time-permits' and/or higher-ups crackle the whip as a ritual.

EXHIBIT 8.2

Innovation : Assessing the Current Status: A Self Appraisal

Note:

a. Please answer the questions in Sl. Nos. 1 to 24.
b. Answers are not meant to gauge your knowledge.
c. Answers are not meant to record of how you wish the things to be or how things are ought to be as per you.
d. Answers are to reflect your judgement based on your experience of the current status.
e. Kindly furnish your answers on a separate sheet giving reference to the Sl. No. of the question.
f. You are also welcome to add new ones to this check-list and also furnish your answers to them.

1. Is bringing out 'changes' for the better, an organisation practice in every department?
2. Are "changes" customer-focused?
3. Give at least three examples of changes brought about in any of the four departments you may be aware of, benefiting the 'customer'.
4. Which department is responsible for innovation in product/process/service?
5. Generally at what stage other departments enter into an innovation project? Which are those departments? What is their role?
6. (a) Are there instances of new products/services that are developed but not reaching market?
   (b) What are the main reasons for not reaching market?
7. (a) Are there instances of inordinate delay in new products/services reaching market?
   (b) What are the main reasons for the inordinate delay?

8. (a) Have any patents been taken? How many?
   (b) How many of these have been commercially exploited?
   (c) Give at least five major reasons for not exploiting?
9. (a) Have there been instances of new product recall from market or planned in-house destruction?
   (b) What are the main reasons?
10. Is innovation activity hampered by bureaucratic controls? Enumerate the crippling controls at least five in number within each activity purchase, funds sanctioning, communication etc.
11. How the projects are selected? What are the criteria? Enumerate at least five.
12. Is the priority-ranking of a project stable? Stable : Rarely changed: Frequently changed:
13. What are the reasons for frequent change? How do they arise?
14. How is the reception to commercialise the project by concerned departments.
    Excellent: Good Indifferent Poor:
15. What are the reasons for the ranking given in 14.
16. What are your suggestions to improve the response in case it is not judged 'excellent'.
17. Recapitulate at least 3-4 projects which have succeeded with your participation and involvement. Enumerate at least six main reasons for their success.
18. Likewise enumerate at least six main reasons for the failures as evidenced through at least 3-4 projects that failed.
19. How many ideas/suggestions you thought worthwhile were not tried? What were the reasons for it?
20. How many ideas/suggestions you thought worthwhile were tried? How many succeeded?
21. List at least five instances which reflected the commitment of management to innovation.
22. Likewise list at least five instances reflecting the credibility gap.
23. If you were to guide innovation activities in an organisation how you would proceed? List out at least first six priority items you would take up.
24. On a rough estimate (Guestimate) according to your judgement furnish the following information:

(a) Categorisation of selected projects.

Sl.No.	Project Category	Percentage
1.	Product	
2.	Process	
3.	Service	
4.	Total	100

(b) Classification of Selected Projects(Products/Process/Service)

Sl. No.	Project Classification	Percentage
1.	Entirely new	
2.	Altogether new types but within the same family.	
3.	Same as at present but new range	
4.	Same ones as at present but up-graded ones.	
5.	Total	100

(c) Objective of the project

Sl. No.	Aimed at	Percentage
1.	New Business	
2.	New Performance	
3.	Improvement in Performance	
4.	Creating new concept of value	
5.	Satisfying an existing value a little better.	
6.	Total	100

(d) Decision on Project Selection

Sl. No.	Decision on Project	Percentage
	A. *Selected due to*	
	1. Cost-benefit	
	2. Quality/performance improvement with direct cost-benefit.	
	3. Quality/performance improvement with increase cost.	
	A. Sub-Total	
	B. *Discarded due to*	
	1. Not having any cost benefit	
	2. Paucity of market data about sales potential	
	3. Discouraging estimate of sales volume	
	B. Sub-Total	
	Sub-Total of (A) and (B)	100

(e) Progress of Projects

Sl. No.	Type of progress and action	Percentage
	1. Encouraging results, project continued.	
	2. Results not very encouraging still continued with hope.	
	3. Results not at all hopeful but still continued.	
	4. Results least encouraging and project stopped.	
	5. Encouraging results, but project stopped.	
6.	Total 100	

(f) Time Utilisation

1. Right ones	
2. Connected but need not have spent time.	
3. Not connected but spent time.	
4. Total	100

EXHIBIT 8.3

How is our Innovation Environment : A Self-Evaluation

Note: Put "X" mark under the appropriate category for each characteristic.

Sl. No.	Characteristic Description	Description and actual situation are*			
		A	B	C	D
1.	No tolerance of inaction				
2.	No 'Committee approach' sit, think, debate, report.				
3.	Key-thought 'move': try, test, quick and dirty.				
4.	Gather resource people, team them, hammer out solution.				
5.	High tolerance for failure of a good and honest try.				
6.	No tolerance of failure due to fraud, irresponsible action, negligence, hollow bravery.				
7.	Failures met with, prior to achieving success, are freely spoken about and made a common knowledge.				
8.	Persons at the top, persons often promoted are the ones known for genuine failures, foul-ups, embarrassments — all encountered in the task taking 'IT to market'.				
9.	Failure is investment in learning Lessons of failure are learnt well and fully made use of.				
10.	Same or similar type of failures do not occur.				
11.	Team approach is practised with conviction and as an easy routine.				
12.	Team members are drawn from different functional groups relevant to the project.				
13.	Customers/suppliers have also a place in the team.				

* A : Close, B : Near, C : Distant, D : Far Out

	A	B	C	D
14. Team is a working, performing, doing entity on a whole time basis. Its concern is to take 'IT to market'.				
15. Team is small in number and under pressure of dead-lines to meet.				
16. Access to information and support is easy.				
17. Open disrespect for petty bureaucracy is shown.				
18. 'Notes/minutes' are least; 'No action, in spite of my note' attitude non-existent.				
19. Ideas are encouraged from all levels.				
20. No idea is considered useless or silly; no idea is allowed to die a premature death.				
21. Senior management's support and encouragement to innovation is seen in their communication as well as action.				
22. Procedures and practices that inhibit and stifle innovation are always taken due care of and modified suitably.				
23. Individuals with an enquiring mind who challenge the assumptions, threaten status-quo and take-risks are encouraged.				
24. Risk-takers and achievers get promotions and recognition.				
25. Active effort is there to identify and encourage people who have a flair to be creative.				
26. Senior management's role in innovation activity is that of a facilitator and contributor not controller or evaluator.				
27. Departmental structure are less rigid and not encapsulated, facilitating free communication and collaboration between departments on innovation projects.				
28. There is periodic exposure to techniques for stimulating and cultivating creativity; enhancing creative ability through seminars, special workshops, creative exercises and games.				

9

SKILLS TO BE INNOVATIVE: Qualitative Attributes

Skills Classification

In this and the following chapter certain skills which help one to develop innovativeness are discussed. 'Flash of genius', powerful intuition and such other intellectual abilities are normally associated with invention. For the present, it may not be possible to acquire them to be endowed with. This aspect is not necessarily a predominant factor as remarkable innovation significant in many ways are taking place at a fast rate in many an enterprise inspite of men/women of 'eminence' being not there. This implies that there are many acquirable concepts, methods, tasks, practices and skills to enhance the innovative abilities of an enterprise as well as individuals. Such acquirable assets as applicable to an enterprise as well as individuals have been discussed in the earlier chapters. There are a few more skills which are "perhaps" are of greater relevance to individuals. These are classified into two categories – skills as qualitative attributes and skills through techniques. This chapter deals with qualitative attributes.

Qualitative Attributes

Innovation, as defined earlier, is the task of taking 'IT' to market and achieving market impact. This task involves extensive networking and criss-crossing with different functional groups. It is a kind of organic process characterised by raising numerous questions; seeking/creating a future for IT in the environment; articulating to make the environment accept the 'IT' and the consequential changes that are brought forth; bestowing adequate attention to implant 'IT' in market to ensure its impact. These characteristics of the process can be matched well if certain qualitative skills are acquired. It helps success in an innovation activity. These skills are classified for ease of understanding and acquiring as insight, vision, versatility and focus. Each one of these is dealt with in this chapter. Traits of each attribute are enumerated to study, ponder over, acquire and adopt.

Insight

Insight in the context of innovation is the ability to raise questions, seek new problems, find solutions, thrive on new ideas, encourage discussion and disagreements for enhancing understanding. It is an aid to generate more 'ITS', make them robust and relevant to market and thus enhance their potential to achieve market-impact. Traits that constitute insight and enhances ones insight are listed in Exhibit 9.1.

Vision

Vision in general is creating future. For innovation, vision means providing a path for an 'IT' to enter market. Path to create future are indicated by the current events, facts, hopes, threats, opportunities, fears and dangers. Thus vision relies on the effective use of the results of an environment-scanning exercise covering social, economic, political, technology, industrial, market etc. A powerful vision brings forth an enterprise and an equally powerful one lifts it to heights of all round achievement. By the same taken of logic the enterprise can fall on the path of neglect and decay with the passing away of the vision behind it leaving nothing to take its place. This highlights the importance of the continuity of vision for continued success and survival of an enterprise. Traits of vision are listed in Exhibit 9.2.

Versatility

Capability to adapt to and adopt changes is versatility. Entry of an 'IT' to market implies certain changes in the methods, customs, practices, attitudes of market and customers. Unless market and customers are tuned, persuaded and convinced of adopting such changes, the chances of an 'IT' succeeding in the market becomes remote inspite of its intrinsically high advantages. Many of the product failures in the market is not due to the product by itself but market not being able to adapt the changes that are involved in the use of new product. Thus, there is need to ensure 'close-fit' between an 'IT' and the market/customers it serves. This close-fit can be achieved through managing the changes that an 'IT' implies to market and customers. Versatality is the skill concerned with this task of achieving close-fit.

To change and adopting to change are not easy. Resistance, fear, prejudices, tradition, caution, avoidance, threat are the barriers to change. Versatility has to cope with all these and bring in an environment to welcome change, adopt change, love change. Traits and characteristics of versatility are in Exhibit 9.3.

Focus

'IT' enters the market. 'Changes' implied are managed well for an 'IT' to get established. These are not enough. Close attention, follow up action are needed to ensure that the 'IT' makes its impact on the market and attains its full maturity. Apart from this, in the wayward path that innovation is right from converting the 'idea' into an 'IT' as a hardware; building and testing the proto-type; rebuilding, if need be; repeating the cycle a few times and entering the market close attention, follow up and flow of resources are necessary at each stage to achieve the overall success. This close attention and direction of efforts involved is called 'focus'. Relevant points concerning this are in Exhibit 9.4.

Amalgam

For clarity and ease of understanding, dissection helps. For unity of purpose, action and achieving, integration is the key. Thus in the above brief discussion each of the skills insight, vision, versatality and focus has been individually dealt with to understand and acquire the skills. But in practice, every innovator has to be an amalgam of all the four using each one adaptively as per the needs and demands. All the four are equally important although their need and demand may vary at a given point of time. An innovation team with an amalgam of these skills in every member of the team can ensure many of the 'ITs' on its hand a resounding success.

EXHIBIT 9.1

Characteristics – Insight

Behavioural pattern of an executive with 'insight' and required to infuse 'insight' are as follows:

- Lover of ideas, enthusiastically goes about understanding the new ideas; anxious about using them; follows up till reaching a logical conclusion.
- Raises questions; number of questions raised are more than the number answered; facilitates to get a better understanding of the idea and problems associated with it.
- Discussions are in the open with all concerned; one up manship is discouraged; free flow of information and discussion are encouraged to generate good understanding, healthy disagreement and formulate appropriate course of positive action.
- The precept that 'no idea is silly' is widely made known. Hence prior to expressing an idea no stress and strain is involved.
- Discourages the tendency to maintain status quo and seek protection that a well established 'tradition' does give.
- Concerned more with performance than conformance to tradition.
- Provides adequate protection against – 'criticism' arising out of doing something new and not as per tradition.
- Does not use parameters like 'logic' 'precision' 'not being simple' 'not practicable', 'not efficient' etc. to shelve and stifle an idea.
- Helps the idea to blow well supporting it through all the work and experimentation involved.

EXHIBIT 9.2

Characteristics – Vision

Work pattern of an executive having 'vision' is as follows:

- Has enough time, patience, energy to discuss things.
- Part of a team, spends most of the time in the work place where 'new things' are being done, and shaped.
- Has a concept of his own on how to organise, make things work, eliminate bottlenecks, move fast, achieve goals.
- Shares his views and concepts on these with colleagues, interacts and puts them to practice.
- Appeal and approach to people are directed at their head and heart as well.
- Has close regular contact with shop floor by wandering about.
- Is communicative, supportive and warm to men of ideas and action.
- 'Builds on strength' and makes weaknesses irrelevant.
- For work and progress departments are no bar, levels of people are no bar.
- 'Blast the mountain and dam the river' marks his limits of vision, tenacity of purpose and pooling of resources.

EXHIBIT 9.3

Characteristics – Versatality

Consideration of the following issues, thinking on them, working on them enhances versatality.

1. Identifying the critical components of the environment that are of relevance to the enterprise.
2. Understanding how the critical components influence the working of the enterprise in terms of its revenue and expenditure.
3. What is the 'state-of-the-art' in the industry to which the enterprise belongs to?
4. How close is the enterprise to 'state-of-art'? What steps are to be taken to reach it?
5. Who are our competitors? What are their names?
6. Who are our customers? What do they want? Are we supplying what they want?
7. What are the threats to our products:

   .. change in the practices of customers
   .. altogether new substitute taking over our products like glass by plastics.
   .. statutory rules/regulations.

   How do we face them and when?

8. What are the distinctiveness and special capabilities of the enterprise:

   .. product
   .. customer service
   .. distribution net work.
   .. customer relationship.
   .. technology

What opportunities of growth these have? Have they been fully utilised?

9. What are the success of the past? How did we succeed? What are the reasons?
10. What are the failures of the past? How did we fail? What are the reasons?
11. What problems inherited from the past are crippling? How do we protect the future from them?

EXHIBIT 9.4

Characteristics – Focus

Consideration of the following issues, thinking over them working on them enhances the attribute skill - focus:

1. What is the main task? What are the sub-tasks related to it?
2. Who is responsible for completing each task?
3. What are the land-marks in the road to completion of each task?
4. What are the resources needed to reach each land mark and the target date?
5. When are the progress to be reviewed for each task?
6. Have 1 to 5 been evolved through participation of all the concerned persons/departments?
7. Have the plans related 1 to 5 been given to every concerned person?
8. What are the likely events/causes that can disturb the schedule? What preventive measures have to be taken to minimise the disturbance? What alternative measures have to be taken to avoid the adverse effect.

10

SKILLS TO BE INNOVATIVE: Quantitative Tools

Background

Intuition, vision, versatility, knowledge, conjecture etc., are required in innovation. It has been observed in the previous chapter that certain qualitative skills can be developed and acquired through practice. Likewise there are certain quantitative tools that help in sharpening one's analytical and logical abilities also. They help in handling the following types of issues that do arise in innovation projects:

- Are objectives clear, appropriate and unambiguous? These are important to avoid the commonly found situation of finding the 'correct' solution for 'wrong' questions leaving the basic problems unresolved.
- For a given issue have all the facts been logically linked and properly sequenced to facilitate proper understanding of the proposition?
- Facts are numerous. Alternatives can be many. Impact of the Innovation can be far and wide. How does one ensure that 'key' factors or alternatives have been identified to assure maximum impact?
- The famous Newtonian experience of 'apple falling' and 'law of gravity' is there to connect apparently non-connectable/ non-correlative facts to bring a 'new and different one' which an innovation is. How to look for such possibilities in a systematic way?
- Have all the possible ideas been generated on a given project including the 'wild', 'outrageous' and 'impossible' ones? How to generate more ideas?

To meet the above needs there are a number of tools that help in quantitative thinking and understanding. This chapter deals with some of the simple and effective tools. They help to think quantitatively instead of the commonly found pattern based on nouns and adjectives.

Tool Box

Commonly used tools are the following:

1. Check list
2. Brain Storming
3. Stratification
4. Morphological analysis
5. Mind map
6. Pareto analysis
7. Cause-effect diagram
8. Affinity diagram
9. Failure-mode-effect criticality analysis (FMECA)
10. Scenario building
11. Scatter diagram and Attributes association
12. Tree diagram
13. Matrix diagram
14. Force field analysis
15. Attribute listing
16. Relations diagram
17. Process-decision program chart.
18. Matrix data analysis
19. Systems search
20. Synectics
21. Imagery
22. Arrow diagram
23. K.T. Method
24. Lateral thinking
25. Analogy
26. Spread sheet

Scope

Of the several tools listed above only the first 16 are briefly covered. The scope is limited to create an interest and awareness. There are a quite a number of publications which describe the methods in great detail.

Innovation activity has to be there in every functional area for ensuring and improving bottom line results of an enterprise. But the focus has to be on

- product development, modification and improvement to enhance its quality and usefulness to customer;
- ensuring that customer service is always on top gear;
- achieving both faster than competitors and maintaining a

dominating position over them; and
exploitation of innovation as a tool to keep up consistent growth.

Against this background, each of the sixteen tools briefly dealt with in this chapter have been described and illustrated with examples of innovation activity related to quality improvement.

Check List

This is the most commonly used method. It is also referred to as 'count down' system. The technique, essentially consists of listing out all the points in advance that are of relevance to a particular 'issue' and 'checking' against each of them later. For example, the list can be examined for 'importance' of each point and rearranged more meaningfully in accordance with their importance, priority or significance etc.

In the preparation of check list it is better if each member of a project thinks about all the points relevant to an issue say 'market evaluation of the product' and records all the results of his thinking as different points in the form of a list. Pooling all the information from such lists helps to come up with a check list that is exhaustive and appropriate; it helps to consolidate the results of diverse view points and formulate a plan of action.

Check list method is more useful in iterative activities like the following ones common to innovation activities.

– Preparing a brief on an innovation proposal, points to be covered;
– Screening of a chemical, general list of characteristics;
– safety clearance for a chemical, list of questions to be examined.

Exhibits 10.1 (a) to 10.1 (c) illustrate the check list for each of the above respectively.

Checklist 'mind-set' is very handy in working out the details of a 'scenario'. It develops a flair for details without missing the sight of larger perspectives. It also inculcates the procedural discipline to check every point of an 'issue' in terms of what it is, against what it ought to be before actually taking up the job.

Brainstorming

The basic requirement for the success of an innovation project is to have a great wealth of ideas to take 'IT' to 'Market' and cause market impact. Traditional methods, practices and approaches may be such that the idea channels are clogged chocked or blocked. There may even be the tendency to feel shy of expressing ideas. An evaluative and judgemental attitude to ideas prevent their very birth. Brain storming is an anti-dote for such situations. The technique owes its origin to A.F. Osborne who invented it "for the sole purpose of producing checklist of ideas that can be used in developing solution to a problem".

The ground rules for brainstorming session to generate ideas are as follows:

a. Identify resource persons known for their ability to generate original ideas or suggestions. The basis for selection is the ability to contribute original ideas/suggestions and not their position in the organisational heirarchy.
b. To conduct the session, select an open-minded, amiable and motivating person from among the coregroup as Chairman and another person with proven ability in communication – written and oral – to record the proceedings of the session.
c. No criticism is permitted. No evaluation or judgemental opinions or views are to be expressed. The floor is free for all members to come out with their ideas.
d. Emphasis is on generating more ideas – quantity and not necessarily quality.
e. Duration of a session can be 60-75 minutes. Chairman facilitates and motivates everyone to come out with ideas.
f. The session starts with a statement of the problem or issue in precise, clear and specific terms giving its background and all relevant information.
g. During the progress of a session and/or subsequent sessions, the specific segments requiring ideas also can be indicated.

If 'ideas rule the world' one of the tools to generate a wealth of ideas is 'Brainstorming'.

Stratification

In the task of taking 'IT' to market, a number of approaches may be available. One may concentrate only in a certain market segment or all segments in a certain area. During the development phase, one may be interested in knowing product failure cause-wise and/or source-wise in order to learn proper lessons out of the past experience. In all these situation there is one common factor and it is 'stratification of information' according to required pattern. Stratification of informaton sharpens the understanding of the problem. Stratification bases are many – material source, machine, operators, time/season, customer, department-wiselike design, manufacturing, quality control etc.

The following presentation of data is an example of two-way stratifiction of information to identify the area of action for improving customer satisfication.

Inwarranty returns of refrigerator compressor in a certain period

Party	Number returned due to						
	Motor burning out	Jamming	Defective pumping	Noisy	Grounded	Other	Total
A	—	2	—	—	1	—	3
B	—	—	1	—	—	—	1
C	—	1	—	—	—	—	1
D	1	6	1	2	—	4	14
E	—	5	1	2	3	1	12
F	7	14	—	5	3	5	34
G	17	26	6	2	5	11	67
Total	25	54	9	11	12	21	132

For pay-off, concentrate on 'jamming' elimination, also on the how and why of high concentration of returns in sources 'G' and 'F'.

Morphological Analysis

This is a very good technique for generation of innovative ideas from a number of variables and their sub species. The term 'morphology' is used in Zoology and Botany to indicate the structure of an organism. The concept is very handy in choosing ideas from the set of variables and their subspecies relevant to the problem.

For example consider the problem of formulating specification for container for a new kind of liquid detergent. Then, the main variables are size, shape, material, closing mechanism, colour etc. There are several choices for each of these variables. The structure of these variables and their species can be set out in a table as below:

Parameters/ Variables and (No. of choices).	Choice type				
Size (litres) (6)	1/4	1/2	1	2	5	10
Shape (5)	Cylindrical	Square	Spherical	Triangular		Jug
Material (4)	Glass,	Special paper,		PVC,	Tin	
Colour (5)	Blue,	Green,	White,	Cream,	Yellow	

To identify the feasible – combinations the following procedure is adopted:

(a) Of the several choices available for each parameter, identify the ones that can be ignored without prejudicing the needs of market.

For the case on hand the results may be as follows eliminating the rest.

.. Size : 1/4, 1/2 1 and 2 (lts)

.. Shape : Cylindrical, Square, Spherical

.. Material : Special paper, PVC

.. Colour : Blue, Green, White;

(b) This reduces the choices from the original 600 (6X5X4X5) combinations to 72 (4X3X2X3) and it is only necessary to formulate the specifications to containers in four sizes; three shapes; two types for materials, and the specific shades in each of three colours.

It is necessary that all the parameters and the different possible choices for each parameter are taken due note of to ensure that nothing of value is omitted. Similarly, in the elimination process there is need to ensure that only the non-worthy ones have in fact been eliminated. The reasons for elimination also must be kept on record for future reference and guidance. This entire exercise is also a group activity involving marketing, manufacturing, design, R&D, and QC and possibly even lead customers/dealers.

Mind Map

An idea is generated or a problem is identified. The next step is to get a wealth of information associated with it. At this stage, the open endedness and free-flow of information without necessarily restricting its type and direction are a must. This process is facilitated by the tool 'mind map'. Its illustration is given in Exhibit 10.2. It is adopted iteratively to refine and zero-down on the few specific relevant and priority ones.

The effectiveness of mind map is of a very high order to solve 'internal' problems through arriving at reasoned consensus. It is one of the simplest accessories available to achieve consensus on the basis of which 'experts' can develop their 'ITs'. These will have a better chance of getting accepted by internal customers.

As in the case of brain storming, mind map session is also a group activity subjected to same ground rules.

Pareto Analysis

Italian economist Vilfredo Pareto at the turn of the last century observed during his study of distribution of wealth that 80-90 per cent of Italy's wealth lay in the hands of 10-12 per cent of its population.

This is found to be a universal law referred to as "ABC analysis" (80-90% the of consumption value of materials is accounted by only about 4-5% of the items); "law of vital few and trivial many" (80-90% of the rejections is attributed to 5-6 causes out of many), "law of vital few and useful many" (80-90% of the sales turnover is accounted by 10-15% of the customers). It is of wide applicability in locating the 'few' out of the many that account for a "major chunk" of the point of interest.

These few merit review, investigation, analysis and critical evaluation. They are the ones that need to be controlled, mended, manipulated, altered, checked to produce a quantum-change in response. The tabulation of data that facilitates the identification of the vital few is called "Pareto Analysis". Exhibit 10.3 gives an illustration.

Cause-effect-diagram

Prof. Kaoru Ishikawa the father of quality circles in Japan designed this method and it is named after him as 'Ishikawa Diagram". It is also called 'fish-bone-diagram'.

The basic purpose of this tool is to facilitate analytical thinking about the causes for a certain effect; categorisation of causes into major factors and sub-factors within a major factor; linking up causes with the effect as a logical network to picturise clearly the entire cause-effect anatomy of the problem.

This is an aid to systematically enumerate all the causes and not leave out anything; logically categorise them and link them; examine the relative magnitude and influence the effect of each cause on the main effect to identify the critical ones and take necessary action on the few critical ones. Exhibit 10.4 gives an illustrative example.

It should be noted that formulating Ishikawa Diagram; going through the motions to identify the few critical/signficant causes are all a group activity involving all the concerned key personnel. At times this exercise brings out the major lapses in facility and/or gaps in knowledge. For example it can even be the case of a critical cause for which no measurement is made or possible much less subjected to control. Thus using cause-effect-analysis can pave way for refining the existing methods, practices, procedure.

Affinity Diagram

This is a creativity mobilisation technique developed by Kawakita Jiro (KJ). Hence it is also called KJ method. The purpose of the method is to generate more ideas, more expressive language as views, suggestions, comments, criticisms and facts to churn out more ideas. This exercise is also organised and conducted on the lines of brainstorming session. When it relates to product development/

improvement lead suppliers/customers/dealers are also to be involved.

The approach consists of enumerating the basic needs to be met by a product in terms of its broad generic classification applicable to a product and inviting various ideas under each generic classification. The grouping of the various ideas under the different generic titles is the affinity diagram. This forms the basis for eventual actions related to formulating product specification, manufacturing standard, material specification etc. Thus for example, the affinity diagram for "brief case" can be as follows:

Cost	Security	Appearance space	Design	Colour	Finish
Low cost	Multiple locks	Regal	High volume	Pleasing	Neat
Easy to repair	Easy to operate	Dignified	High utility	Non-fading	Clean
		Space for facilities	Water proof		No projections
		Easy to reach	Moth proof		Name tag
		Easy to recognise	Pilfer proof		Light weight
		Accommodating	Strong hinges		Strong handle
		one day needs of warm/ winter clothing	Withstanding abuses		Unbreakable
			Long lasting		
		Elegant	Serving as pillow		Takes polish
			Non-staining		
			Scratch proof		
		Tough			

Failure mode effect and Criticality analysis (FMECA)

The following points have been mentioned in the earlier chapters on 'failure' in the context of innovation:

(a) Failure is not a dirty word but a welcome event for improving knowledge and understanding.
(b) More failures must be generated deliberately under diverse condtions to develop a robust reliable product.

In addition to the above, it is necessary to have an assessment of the criticality of each type of failure to help in developing a robust reliable product.
FMECA is a technique that helps to arrive at criticality index as risk priority number (RPN). Higher the value of RPN associated with a component greater is its criticality and hence more attention is needed to render it failure free. Exhibit 10.5 gives an illustration of the technique and following are the definitions associated with the technique.

a. *Failure mode*: This pertains to the physics of failure in terms of form and manner of failure; location and mechanics of failure. The details give enough clues as to the manner in which the failure can be prevented through strengthening of materials by changing dimensions and/or material itself; reducing stress, strain, wear and tear etc. through proper devices, outlets to dissipate energy, heat, pressure, friction etc, developed during usage; harmonising interfacing fits and tolerances etc. Failure mode is assessed on a numerical scale for each failure ranging from 1 to 10 where one represents low frequency and 10 high frequency of occurrence.
b. *Failure effect*: The effect of failure on the product/service as a whole is in terms of its performance, disruption caused, effect on environment etc. This is also assessed on a scale of 1 to 10 as defined above.
c. *Failure Criticality*: The magnitude of the effect of failure as total loss in terms of safety hazard, loss due to replacement/repair of product. This is measured in terms of difficulty in assessing criticality on a scale from 1 to 10 where '1' represents easy assessment and 10 represents very difficult to assess.

d. *Criticality index or Risk priority number (RPN)*: This is a product of ratings/scores associated with failure mode, failure effect and failure criticality.

FMECA is an effective means for quantifying objectively the criticality of a component failure in a system; sub-system failure in a major system etc.

Scenario Building

In one of the chapters it has been mentioned that developing "future consciousness" through total scanning of the environment is necessary to place an enterprise always in a strong economic position through appropriate and timely action.

It can be one of staying and expanding in the current line of business and/or moving into new ones. The effective tool to facilitate this is 'scenario building'.

Scenario building is not 'nut and bolts' project report, project planning; not an idle poetic dream in an irony tower. It is a concrete exercise to determine the 'direction' in which an enterprise is to be navigated; types of actions needed to be taken now for what an enterprise going to be in the next say 3 or 5 years to stay fit economically. This is not a one time exercise but a continuous one and the inputs are hard realities, knowledge, results of environmental scanning, vision and gut feeling.

Thus for example in our country, TVS deciding to manufacture automobile accessories when they were well reputed, entrenched and established dealers and service agents of automobile accessories is an example of scenario building. It consisted of having identified in advance that the direction and area of navigation, growth and consolidation lies in itself becoming a manufacturer of automobile accessories. Which item, where, when, mode of financing, collaboration etc, are matters of "nuts and bolts" project planning that comes later after determining the direction of navigation.

Yet another example is that of ITC in having, visualised that it has to enter the "Tourism Industry' and 'edible oil' even while it was strong in its traditional field.

Yet another example is that of Royal Dutch/Shell which under the patriarch of its scenario planning, Peter Schwartz's advice, invested a huge fortune in developing natural gas deposits off the coast of Norway reaping rich harvest. The patriarch of scenario planning foresaw perestroika in 1983 (when powerful nations still perceived USSR as an 'evil empire', Michail Gorbachev as yet another obscure official); and thus felt convinced there would be no difficulty due to Russian influence on marketing of what could prove to be gas of Russian origin.

"The end result of Scenario planning is not an accurate picture of tomorrow", "Rather it is to help oneself change ones view of reality – to match it up more closely with reality as it is and reality as it is going to be".

Scatter Diagram and Attributes – Association

There arises the need to examine the relationship between a 'factor' and 'response'. It may be temperature, pressure, or ph etc, the 'factor' influencing yield, purity or concentration etc, the 'reponse'.

Readily available data from process log-books, laboratory analysis will be of immense use in examining the live-situation. Use of scatter diagram and attributes – association will be helpful in these types of exercise.

Figure 10.1 illustrates the example of a scatter diagram. Pairs of data on 'factor' and corresponding 'response' are plotted on a graph paper. If the plotted data were to be such that response progresses in a certain direction with progression in the values of the factors as in figure 10.1, it prima-facie indicates that an empirical relationship may exist. Statistical methods are available to test its validity as not arising out of 'chance' and also determine the empirical, equation, in the case of figure 10.1 the straight line equation, between 'factor' and 'response'. It helps to locate the range within which factor needs to be controlled so as to maximise the response.

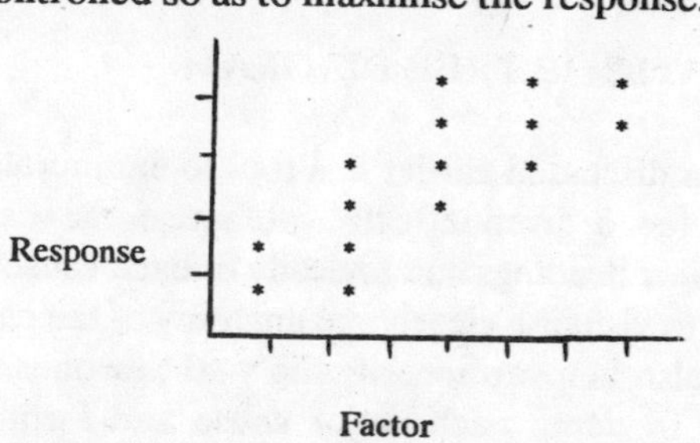

Fig. 10.1: Scatter diagram

When natural paired data are not available, attribute association is applicable. This can handle more than one factor/response. Attribute association method is illustrated in the following example:

a. Factors considered	:	Two say A (Temp. °C) and B (Pressure PSI).
b. Response considered	:	Two say X (Purity) and Y (yield)
c. Grouping the factors	:	A into say A_1(75-80) A_2 (80-85)A_3 (85-90).
		B into say B_1 (100-105) B_2 (105-110) B_3(110-115)
		X into X_1(60-65)X_2 (65-70) X_3 (70-75)
		Y into Y_1 (80-85)Y_2 (85-90) Y_3 (90-95)

Scrutiny of the available data would help in the above classification.

d. Frequency recording (from basic-data viz. plant log)	:	Record the frequency of occurence of X_1, X_2 and X_3 in each of the nine cells (3 of Ax3 of B) and summarise the information as in Table 10.1. Likewise repeat for Y and summarise the information as in Table 10.1.

e. Identify the area of interest, if any, in Table 10.1.

SYSTEMATIC OR TREE DIAGRAM

Cause and effect diagram discussed earlier is a tool to enumerate all the causes responsible for a given effect; categorise the causes according to different major headings and logically fit each cause into the appropriate heading to visualise clearly the anatomy of the causes influencing an effect. It also helps to identify the vital few ones. The next task is to examine in depth each major cause and formulate suitable course of action. This is largely facilitated through the total systematic or tree diagram and it is illustrated in Exhibit (14).

TABLE 10.1: Attribute – Association

Frequency of occurrence of X_1 X_2 X_3 in different ranges of A and B in the basic data:

Factor range B	Factor range A: A_1			A_2			A_3			Total		
	X_1	X_2	X_3	X_1	X_2	X_3	X_1	X_2	X_3	X_1	X_2	X_3
B_1	2	3	2	7	4	6	3	6	4	12	13	12
B_2	4	4	6	1	8	8	2	10	12	7	22	26
B_3	10	12	6	4	15	12	4	18	18	18	45	36
Total	16	19	14	12	27	26	9	34	34	37	80	74

Note:

1. From the above table it can be seen that frequency of response in higher ranges are concentrated in the region covered by the four corner points B_2-A_2, B_2-A_3 and B_3,- A_2, B_3-A_3.
2. Statistical significance of this apparent concentration can be assessed.
3. Detail 'probing' can be done further in the area of concentration after establishing statistical significance.
   'Probing' can mean design of experiments, EVOP application etc.

Matrix Diagram

Consider the following situations:

- How to find a product from among the several ones available, the one that fits well to a given market segment?
- How to find a process/method from among the several ones possible, the one that is suited for a given task?
- How to find a strategy from among the different available alternatives, the one that is most appropriate to achieve a given set of objectives?

Each of these problems is different. But to find the answers to the problem involved in each case, there is a common approach. This is the tool of 'matrix diagram' comprising of the following steps:

- Identify the 'frame' and the 'thing' that has to fit into the frame. In the above cases, the frame is market segment, task and set of objectives; the corresponding 'thing' is product, process/ method, strategy.
- Characterise the 'frame' in detail in terms of its characteristics.
- Assign a score-cum-symbol for each characteristic. It can be "score of five" - * - "excellent", 4-**-very good; 3-a-good; "1-aa-average" and 'zero-x-not useful'.
- Take each candidate of the thing. Evaluate its association with every characteristic of the frame in terms of its score-cum-symbol. Find the total score. These steps are shown in Exhibit 10.7.
- Choose the candidate with highest score as the best choice of the thing for a given 'frame'.

The candidate thus selected has a better chance of proving to be a success. A review of the profile of its association with the characteristics of the frame indicates the ones that are on the weaker side meriting priority attention and action.

Thus it can be seen that matrix diagram is a tool that saves time involved in making right choices and also it is an effective device to identify the areas to be strengthened in the ones selected.

Force Field Analysis

Kurt Lewin a social psychologist developed this method. It is based on the following concept that a given goal can be attained through building on 'strengths', rendering 'weakness' irrelevent and taking simultaneous actions on both.

In the task of achieving a certain objective/goal, at any given point of time there would be positive forces helping to achieve targets and also the negative ones acting as a drag. These negative forces are not necessarily 'human problems'. They can arise out of certain other limitations also. When negative forces dominate, it can dampen the interest and drive out of the enthusiasm behind a venture resulting in its failure. To avoid such situations 'force-field' approach is recommended. It comprises of the following and an illustration is given Exhibit 10.8.

- Be always alive to actual situation

- Categorise the forces into two sets, one set of favourable forces and another unfavourable one.
- Ensure that the resultant of these two of opposing forces is always a positive one so that goal is attained.
- To accomplish the above task examine the favourable and unfavourable sets as hereunder.

Favourable	Unfavourable
Identify the critical ones which if strengthened gives a pay-off.	Identify the critical ones which if weakened gives a good relief
Method of strengthening the critical ones Any new force that can be added. Mode of adoption	Method of weakening the critical ones. Which of the forces can be neutralisted? Mode of neutralising.

Force field approach has to be kept in view always. Steps must be taken to ensure that the resultant of positive and negative force is always positive so that goal is achieved. By this approach at no time innovation efforts take a nose dive due to pull of negative forces. Force-field approach has also the virtue of looking at negative forces positively.

Attribute Listing

Innovation as already noted, is achieving something 'new and different' that impacts the market. The different modes of market impact can be categorised as follows:

Product/services	Impacting market	
	Existing	New
Existing types	With new applications	With existing applications with new applications.
New types	With existing applications with newapplications.	With existing applications with new applications

In order to structure the products/services and application to suit existing and new markets it becomes very essential to have a clear knowledge of the following:

- What 'attributes' the products/services should possess?
- What is the status of each attribute as on date?
- How relevant is the attribute to the targetted market?
- What specific issues need to be looked into in each attribute to ensure market impact?
- Develop an inventory of ideas fast and act on the critical ones.

All these aspects can be examined in a systematic way through use of the tool 'attribute listing' as illustrated in Exhibit 10.8. The classical example of attribute listing is that of successful Tarus/Sable programme of Ford that covered 400 features from major performance parameters to the ease with which the gas cap could be removed. The objective was to become the best in class on most of the features and it did achieve in 80 per cent of the features listed.

The acromyn 'SCAMPER' of A F Osborne of brainstorming fame can prove very handy to generate fast action-oriented thoughts where each letter stands for .

S – Substitue
C – Combine
A – Adapt, adopt
M – Modify, magnify, minify
P – Put to other uses
E – Eliminate
R – Reverse, rearrange

RELATION DIAGRAM

This is yet another tool to identify on the basis of logical analysis and linkage of causes associated with a problem, the major causes which help in solving the problem. Relations diagram is a tool of such a logical analysis. It is a diagram in which the problem is represented as a central node. Other nodes representing the causes are directly linked to the central node through arrows. Like-wise it is possible to have a relation diagram for each causal node. The node that has to it multiple linkages is the major factor that merits attention, study and action. This is illustrated in figure 10.2 from where it can be seen that A B C turn out to be the major factors for controlling the defect, poor bonding. They are major ones as they have multiple arrows entering their node on the strength of process logic.

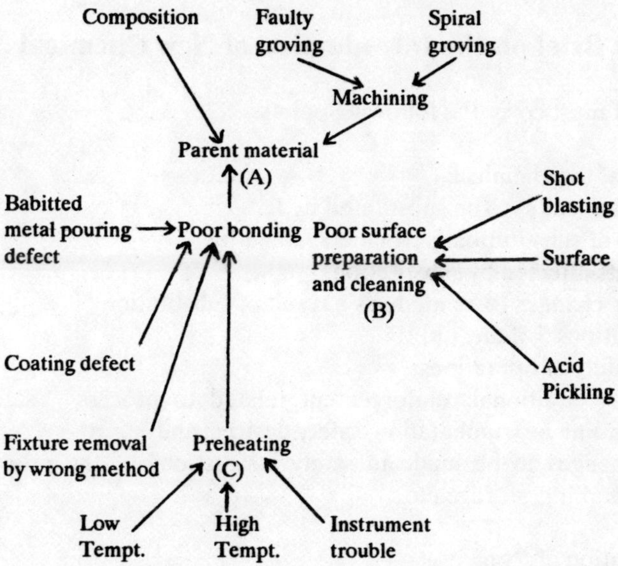

Fig. 10.2: Relation Diagram

EXHIBIT 10.1 (a)

R&D Brief on the Introduction of New Chemical

R&D brief must cover the following points:

1. Name of the chemical.
2. The chemical(s) to be substituted by 1.
3. Nature of substitution: permanent/stand-by.
4. Products affected by substitution.
5. Process changes to be made as a result of substitution.
6. Implications 5, if any on,
   (a) safety of operations;
   (b) any additional reinforcement related to process – safety, on-line instrumentation, safety devices; and
   (c) changes to be made in safety instructions of the process, handling, storage etc.

7. Implication of 5 on:
   (a) production
   (b) quality
   (c) throughput
   (d) effluent
   (e) reinforcement, if any, needed on (a) to (d)
   (f) changes to be made in impacted activities related (a) to (d)

8. Reasons for substitution (quantitative assessment to be given):
   - total cost benefit
   - quality and safety improvement
   - productivity/throughput gain
   - import-sustitution
   - easy availability
   - any other (specify).

9. Who else is using this chemical within and outside the country?
10. Any information available about their experience?

11. If no one is using the material, possible reasons for the same. Could it be that the idea has never struck anyone?
12. Grade recommended for use:
    - pure,
    - technical,
    - analytical,
    - any other (specify)
13. Source of supply:
    - indigenous
    - imported,
    - own manufacture
14. Ultimate chemical form in which used.
15. Role of the chemical in final product system.
16. (a) Is the chemical a hazardous one?
    (b) Have all the properties been known and studied?
    (c) Are facilities available to handle and store it?
    (d) What are the additional facilities, if any, needed to handle, store and use the chemical?
17. (a) What are the quality and safety related characteristics of the product which have been examined?
    (b) What are the results?
    (c) How do they compare with the current ones?

EXHIBIT 10.1 (b)

Generalized List of Characteristics of a Chemical

(1) Visual/Appearance characteristics, odour, structure, foreign matter etc.

(2) Physical characteristics

Melting point (°C)
Particle size/shape
Bulk density (g/cc)
Apparent density (g/cc)
Flow property
Distillation range (Boiling point etc.)
Specific gravity
Softening point/set point
Ignition temperature (°C)

Calorfic value (bomb calorimeter)
Flash point (°C)
Viscosity in cps
Refractive index
Optical density
Miscibility (specify solvent)

(3) Chemical characteristics
Moisture (temperature and time) Hygroscopicity (%RH, time of exposure and temperature).

Chemical purity
Water solubles
Water insolubles
Acid solubles (specify acid)
Acid insolubles (specify acid)
Solvent solubles (specify solvent)
Solvent insolubles (specify solvent)
Acidity (expressed as)

Alkalinity (expressed as)
Ash content
Volatile matter
Residue on evaporation
Grit (a) inorganic (b) organic

(4) Usage characteristics
Flow property
Bulk density
Grain size
Particle shape
Heat test
Chemical stability
Storage sensitivity
Minimum value
Impact sensitivity

Note:
1. This is not an exhaustive list
2. This needs to be updated from time to time
3. In any given case, relevant characteristics must be considered.

EXHIBIT 10.1 (c)

Points to be Examined for Safety-Related Characteristics

(a) Has specification list for the chemical been furnished?
(b) Are all characteristics covered in (a) ?
(c) Has each characterisc the tolerance limit?
(d) Is it free from ambiguity?
(e) Has method of sampling been specified?
(f) Are methods of analysis for each characteristic available? Are they appropriate?
(g) Can all the tests be carried out in our laboratory?
(h) Which analysis cannot be done? What are the implications?
(i) Classify the characteristics according to their significance to cost, quality, safety.
(j) What are the characteristics which can be judged only through performance trials?
(k) Which characteristics are incompatible with other chemicals of the system? What are its implications? What is the method of dealing with them?
(l) Which impurities are altogether forbidden?
(m) What is the effect of different levels of temperature (hot and cold storage) and relative humidity?
(n) What is minimum shelf-life?
(o) What are the storage instructions – relative humidity, minimum quantity to be stored etc?
(p) What are the handling instructions?
(q) What are the packing specifications – type of container, air tightness etc.?
(r) Has the same understanding been reached by every concerned department R&D, Production, QC, Safety, materials with respect to each of the quality/safety/characteristics?

EXHIBIT 10.2

Mind-Map: Broad Outline and Illustration

(a) For a given problem, a number of issues/sub-problems associated with it are represented as a mind map for all to see, proact and deliberate. As illustration, mind map possible for 'high absenteesm' is given in Fig. 1.

(b) On each of the sub-elements of the main problem reach a consensus. This changes the initial mind map. Thus for example, after discussion, it may turn out that providing transport facility does not mitigate the problem and hence can be ignored; priority attention has to be given for positive actions like production incentive and attendance bonus; punitive measures, for chronic cases need to be taken up with firmness etc. On the basis of the consensus thus reached the original map changes reflecting the agreed points.

(c) The mind map approach can be adopted on each of the agreed issues separately to generate the ideas; agree on the core and relevant ones for further action.

(d) It should be noted that mind map approach is to evolve a consensus and not to take away the relevance and importance of experitise involved. Consensus ensures involvement and acceptance of all concerned to the cure 'capsules' formulated by the professionals/experts.

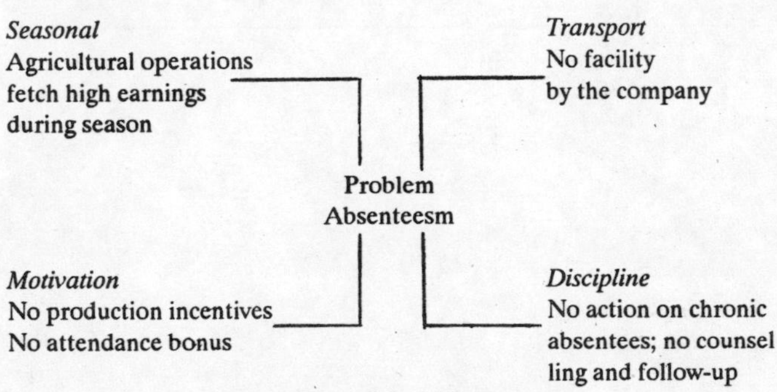

Fig. 1: Mind Map

EXHIBIT 10.3

Pareto Law: Law of Vital Few and Trivial Many

Component	:	Hydraulic cylinder
Problem	:	Rejection at final testing
Causes	:	There are twenty five different causes for rejection
Objective	:	To identify the few vital causes
Procedure	:	Obtain the data on rejections over a period of time cause wise and summarise the data in the form given hereunder in the decreasing order of magnitude. The top few automatically turn out to be 'vital few' of the many causes of rejection. In the present case first six causes out of 25, account for nearly 85% of the rejections.

S.No.	Reason for rejection	No.	Cumulative	% Cumulative
1.	Rod seal leak	69	69	56.1
2.	Port leak	14	83	67.4
3.	Side leak	6	89	72.4
4.	Stroke U/S	6	95	77.2
5.	Collar tight	5	100	81.3
6.	Jerky treatment	4	104	84.6
7.	Plunger tight	3	107	87.0
8.	Bush leak	3	110	89.4
9.	Plug leak	2	112	91.0
10.	Others (16 different causes)	11	123	100.0
		123		

EXHIBIT 10.4

Cause-Effect Diagram : Illustration

"Leak" in refregirator; to identify signficant 'factors'. Here effect is "leak" the "problem of interest", cause is an element contributing to effect.

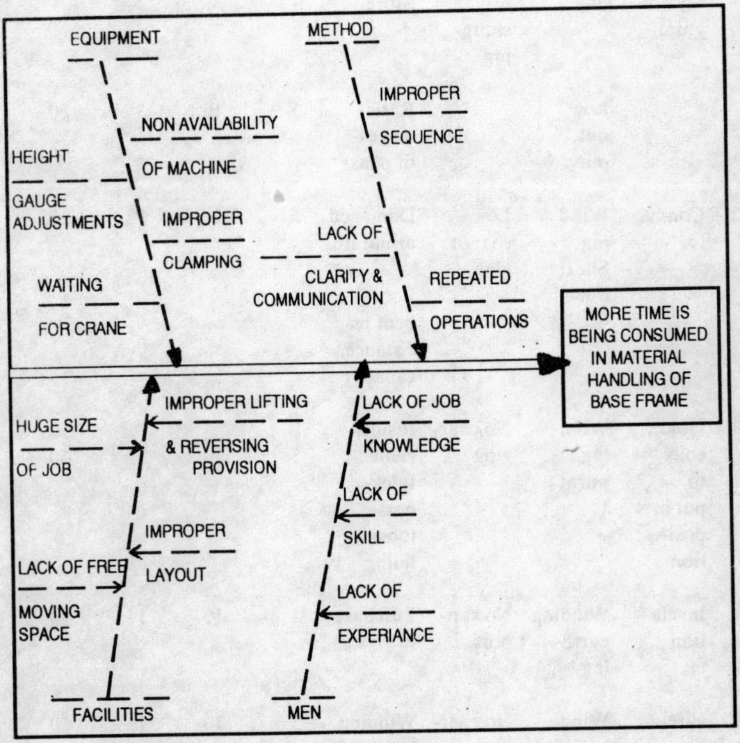

EXHIBIT 10.5

Failure Mode Effect and Criticality Analysis (FMECA)

Dynamo Sub-assembly (S1)

Part	Function	Failure mode	Effect of failure	Cause of failure	Occurrence	Severity	Detection	RPN
(1)	(2)	(3)	(4)	(5)	(6)	(7)	(8)	(9)
S11	Stationary armature	Foulling	No battery charging	ID More	1	10	1	10
		Low out put		Resistance of phase	1	10	3	30
S12	Conductor	Winding Short burnt	Low charging	Damaged armature Poor heat resistance capacity	5	5	7	175
S13	Hold coils to put in position	Winding burnt	No charging	Insufficient thickness loose lining	5	10	1	50
S14	Insulation	Winding earthing	No support	Purchase	1	10	1	10
S15	Effective insulation	Winding short burnt	No charging	Winding loose	5	10	1	50

(a) Past data, experience are used in giving the score. It is better the score is given on the basis of collective wisdom of design, manufacturing, QC, marekting, customer service group and even lead users. Competitors performance is also to be taken due note of.

(b) Based on RPN score corrective actions on S12, S13, and S15 are to be intiated on priority.

EXHIBIT 10.6

Major cause for analysis: Breakage of Mechanical seal

– Tree Diagram illustration.

Level-1	Level-2	Specification	Status	Suggestions
(A) Defective seal	(A_1) Damage during packing	Not given	Not Ok	Formulate packing specification and efforce it.
	(A_2) Poor Design	Design Given	Not given to Vendor	Send drawings to vendor.
(B) Operator skill	(B_1) Rough handling	—	Importance not realised	Characterise correct handling, characterise wrong handling.
Breakage of mechanical seal		—	—	—
	(B_2) Lack of training	—	No training	Notify to all concerned the above; educate and enforce correct method.
(C) Defective matching parts	(C_1) Manufacturing defect	As per drawing	Process capability not OK.	Improve process capability
	(C_2) Inspection errors	As per drawing	Deburring not done, sharp edges not removed	Instruct machine operators to remove sharp edges

EXIBIT 10.7

Matrix diagram - Illustration

'Frame' : Characteristics of an application area 'A' in terms of the type of Ink it needs.

'Thing : Eight different types of ink, I-1 to I-8, each having an equal claim for use in A.

Problem : To select the best among the eight different types of ink that suit well A.

Approach : Matrix-diagram approach for selection is given in the following table.

Score scale : 5-*-excellent; 4-**-very good; 3-a-good; 1-aa- average; and zero-x-not useful.

Characteristics of A		Sl. No.	Evaluation of the strength of association of							
Category	Characteristics		I-1	I-2	I-3	I-4	I-5	I-6	I-7	I-8
Quality	Viscosity	(1)	aa	x	aa	*	**	*	**	*
	Water proofness	(2)	**	**	*	**	a	**	a	x
	Rub Resistance	(3)	*	*	**	**	**	**	**	x
	Drying	(4)	x	x	x	**	**	*	**	aa
	Opacity	(5)	**	*	**	a	aa	aa	aa	x
Compatibility	Drg.pen	(6)	x	x	x	*	aa	*	*	x
	Croquil	(7)	**	x	*	aa	aa	aa	aa	x
	Brush	(8)	a	*	a	x	aa	x	x	x
Suitability	Drg.Paper	(9)	**	x	**	**	**	**	**	a
	Tracing paper	(10)	a	x	x	*	**	*	*	x
	Polyester film	(11)	x	x	x	**	x	*	x	x
	Tracing cloth	(12)	**	x	*	x	*	x	x	x
	Art paper	(13)	x	x	x	*	**	*	**	x
	Writing paper	(14)	x	x	x	**	a	**	a	*
	OHP sheet	(15)	x	a	x	a	x	a	x	x

Total of		Evaluationof the strength of association of							
		I-1	I-2	I-3	I-4	I-5	I-6	I-7	I-8
Excellent	(*)	1	3	3	4	1	6	2	2
very good	(**)	5	1	3	6	6	4	5	—
good	(a)	2	1	1	2	2	1	2	1
average	(aa)	1	—	1	1	4	2	2	1
not useful	(x)	6	10	7	2	2	2	4	11
Total score	—	32	22	31	51	39	51	38	14

I-4 and I-6 are the right candidates for further action. Profile of their association with individual characteristics indicates that there is scope of improve w.r.t Sl. No.(8) and (12). Cost of I-4 and I-6 is also yet another dimension to be examined.

Thus it can be seen that matrix diagram helps to select the right ones from among the several alternatives available besides throwing up many right questions for examination and action.

Note: (1) Score is obtained as under:
No. of '*' X 5 plus No. of '**' X 4
plus No. of 'a' X 3 plus No. q 'aa' X 1
plus No. of 'x' X Zero.

(2) It is obvious that in giving the score knowledge and experience play a key-role.

EXHIBIT 10.8

Force field approach – illustration

Problem	: It releates to a case of handling heavy cargo containers of 25 T and above. Cargo containers come in trucks. A set of 6 fork lifts, three on either side of the truck work in perfect harmony and understanding to lift the container from the truck, allow the truck to move out and then slowly lower down the cargo container to rest on the ground to remove the contents from the containers. To entire operation is highly risky and hazardous to drivers, fork lift operators, cargo container and cargo itself.
Goal	: To improve safety.
Force field	: Forces acting on the field of safety were categorisded as under.

Positive forces	*Negative forces*
. Knowledgeable workmen	. Heavy duty fork lift not available.
. Work-crew well motivated	. Cargo had to be handled using a pack of lifts with a total capacity matching the needs of cargo and individual capacity of each lift being far less.
. Work crew not tradition bound	
. Harmony in work crew	
. Safety concious	. Resources not available to purchase/lease heavy duty fork lifts.

Categorisation showed that pay off lines in neutralising the negative forces by questioning the basic "mind-set" issues –

Is heavy duty lift at all necessary? Is handling the container warranted at all? Raising right questions brought into sharp focus the realities thus:

(a) *the thing* needed is to unload the material contained in the container.
(b) all other activities are secondary.
(c) material can be removed directly from the container the same way it was put in the container.
(d) capacity of each of the available fork lift is more than adequate to handle the material and
(e) no need to handle the container.
(f) no need to buy heavy duty fork lifts.

Accordingly the practice was changed to (c) on the strength of (d). Positive forces facilitated the quick adoption and assimilation; sources of risk and hazard were totally eliminated.

EXHIBIT 10.9

Attribute listing – Illustration

Product : Domestic refregirator *Purpose* to market in a new area

S.No.	Attributes	Relevant issues to be examined
1.	Size	How many sizes ? Is there anything new to be introduced for the proposed area? Has there been a product-size distribution profile?
2.	Shape	Similar issues as Sl. No. (1)
3.	Colour	Similar issues as Sl. No. (1)
4.	Maintenance free features (customer oriented)	What changes over the prsent? – Enumerate for each.
	– Door closure Mechanism	Do they really "experience" them? How do they come to know the superiority of the features?
	– Linings/ insulation	
	– Defrosting	
	– Fasteners/ anchoring	
	– Self closure devices	
	– Cocroach/moth proofness	
	– Accessibility for cleaning	
	– Ease of cleaning	
ETC.		

11

INNOVATION AND STABILITY

Background

So far the subject of innovation has been discussed right from its definition to the skills to be innovative. The primary purpose of innovation is to achieve "stability". This chapter discusses the subject of innovation and stability along with certain related issues.

Innovation

The very expression innovation connotes change. At times a change in the environment leads to innovation. A felt-need of the market leads to innovation of a new product. This is an instance of environment-induced innovation. In contrast to this, there is also the case of innovation changing the environment. Plastic pot replacing the metallic one is a case of innovation changing environment.

The central point to be noticed is that innovation symbolises a state that disturbs the *status quo*, induces new adaptations and calls for absorption of new things.

Stability

Stability is there where interruptions are far and few. Then, how could innovation and stability co-exist? Is it not a paradox? Yes, it is a paradox. Co-existence of innovation and stability seems contradictory but in fact they co-exist as innovation induces and sustains stability. But the question is stability of what? It is the stability of economic performance,bottom line results, of an enterprise.

It has already been noted that the survival and success of an enterprise in a fast changing business environment is essentially dependent on its ability to sense the changes/developments that are under way, understand their significance and take suitable measures to adopt/adjust to the changes to ensure economic stability. The adaptive process is innovation.

By the same token of argument, an enterprise which is immune or slow to react to environmental changes gets out of focus, dips its performance and throws itself into a state of economic instability.

The above points are summarised in Table 11.1.

TABLE 11.1: Stability of Activities vs Stability of Enterprise in a Changing Environment

Activities say related to products, process, customer services	Stability of the Enterprise
Consistently changing to meet customer & market needs	Stable; growth and profit can be maintained and improved upon.
Stable and unchanging	Unstable; growth and profit are threatened and can decline.

It is not enough if the activities of an enterprise are constantly changing to meet the needs of the customer and market. It is more important that the changes also must take place with speed to take an "IT" to market ahead of the competitors. This will be a crucial factor in the years ahead.

In order that innovation process is always focused on right issues, an enterprise has to consistently remind itself of how the environment is; what transformations are needed in its different functional areas; and how the enterprise is judging its adaptiveness to changes; and how it is strengthening innovation activity on a total basis. These are briefly discussed in this chapter.

Environmental Factors

It is necessary to keep a track of developments that are taking place in the following key areas (illustrative and not exhaustive) and understand relevancy of these developments to enterprise and take suitable measures:

– Governamental policies; fiscal; industrial; licence; quota, control and distribution; duty, tariffs and subsidies, etc.

- Manufacturing technology to increase variety and volume to shrink cycle time from design to reaching customer.
- Use of information technology in all areas to strengthen networking with purchasing, suppliers, design, manufacturing, product support, distribution, customer and market etc.
- Business mergers and take overs.
- Political developments and social upheavels.
- Market segmentation, product preferences and needs.

The means of 'scanning' are diverse. To name a few, they are patents published, journals, news letters and information digests relevant to the industry; government gazettes and notifications; bills before parliament and the likely ones to be introduced; industry seminars, conferences and workshops; discussions with peers experts and knowledgeable persons/consultants.

The most important segment of scanning also relates to sources of 'threat' for the enterprise. Thus for example, an enterprise in glassware manufacture, needs to keep track of developments in plastics; steel to track aluminium etc.

Apart from these a good association with lead users and lead customers also provide valuable information on threats and opportunities.

Transformation in Different Functional Areas

Every functional area has to undergo certain transformations in order to cope with the change. This reinforces the point already stated that innovation is a plant wide activity in every functional group not merely associated with products, process and technology. The typical transformations needed in different functional areas are in Exhibit 11.1.

Adaptiveness - A Method for Evaluation

It is necessary to assess and evaluate how adaptive are the key activities of an enterprise to meet the needs of the day. One such method is to:

- review and evaluate the changes/modifications introduced over a period of time in different functional areas as listed in exhibit 11.2.

- Ensure that where changes/modifications have been few over the years, they have not caused or imply *no adverse* effect on the enterprise.
- Assure that where changes/modifications have been fairly good over the years, they have been necessary and beneficial to the enterprise; also identity the ones that are not so and the reasons there for.

Such an evaluation helps to direct the innovation activities on proper lines. Format given in Exhibit (19) can be used for review and evaluation of changes over a period of time.

Organic Factors that Strengthen Innovation

Innovation process as a means to achieve economic stability has been dealt with. Method of evaluation of the adaptiveness of an enterprise in every functional area to meet the changing needs of the environment has been covered.

There are certain organic factors which must be enriched in an enterprise to strengthen the innovation process itself. Some of these have been dealt with in the earlier chapters. A few more key factors that need to be taken due note of, enriched and practised by every enterprise to strengthen its innovation base and capability are in Exhibit 11.3.

EXHIBIT 11.1

Transformations Needed in Different Functional Areas

Sl. No.	Functional area	What it is now typically	Transformation needed
1	2	3	4
1.	Leadership	.. Detached .. Analytical .. Centralised Strategy .. Planning .. Driven by corporate staff	.. Lover of change .. Preacher of vision and shared valves. .. Strategy development through grass root. .. Staff functions support line-function not vice versa
2.	Structure	.. Heirarchical .. Functional integrity maintained .. People need tight control .. People specialise but diminish their role. .. Guarding the turf, priority concern. .. Conformance to 'Rule book'.	.. Flat .. Functional barriers broken .. First-line superiors give way to self managed teams. .. Middle managers as facilitators rather than turf guardians. .. 'Performance' not conformance to rules book.
3.	Purchasing/ Procurement of raw materials and components.	.. Inspect and accept .. Rigid control on supplier .. Contractual and legalistic bordening on adversarial relationship.	.. Develop supplier .. Supplier is a business partner promoting quality image. .. No over dependence- on acceptance - inspection.
4.	Workforce	.. Adversarial: Labour and management.	.. Participative, self managing. . Sharing of informa-

Contd.

1	2	3	4
		.. No sharing of information .. Restricted role .. Demanding 'more': labour as well as management of their own interest	tion, a must. .. Wider role in planning, for quality, safety, meeting, targets, meeting delivery schedules solving shop problems etc.
5.	Manufacturing	.. Emphasis on volume, cost, functional integrity. .. Concern for meeting the plan given. .. Score-board on 'quantity produced' is all important.	.. Quality becoming primary marketing tool. .. Responsiveness, and innovation of high order. .. Part of product design team from the start. .. Shrinking 'cycle-time' from concept to supply. .. Short runs, flexibility, automation supporting people.
6.	Financial management	.. Centralised .. Finance staff as Cop. .. Multiple levels of control and approval.	.. Decentralised .. Finance people as "business team members". .. High spending authority down the line.
7.	Management information	.. Internally focused .. Centralised for the sake of consistency	.. Decentralisation .. Key link up points: supplier and customer. market, distribution.
8.	Training	.. No planned programmes to develop personnel;	.. Continuous training of personnel; programmes to sensi-

Contd.

1	2	3	4
		.. Treated as optional.	tise on future consciousness; to develop skills to manage "new and different".
9.	Cost	.. Rising too rapidly making it difficult to sustain product prices.	.. Reduction in quality losses like wastage, excess consumption, rework etc. .. Reduction in non-productive expenditure. .. Rationalisation of man power.
10.	Quality Assurance	.. Inspection intensive .. Response only when demanded by external agencies confined to products only. .. Large inspection staff.	.. Quality management as plant wide activity. .. Quality covers products and services. .. Smell of quality is felt and experienced by customer at all places of the enterprise.
11.	Marketing	Mass markets .. Mass advertisements .. Concern on market share .. Battles to increase market share.	.. Niche focus .. Innovation for being closer to markets and customer. .. Thriving on market creation. .. Ceaseless differentiation of any product inspite of its high maturity.

Contd.

1	2		3		4
				..	Reach market fast to out smart the competitors.
				..	Build on customer services.
12.	International	..	Meant for big firms only.	..	Essential strategy for firms of all sizes.
13.	Sales and service	..	"Move-the-product" is the dominating	..	Heroes
				..	Relationship of management with every customer.
				..	Major source of ideas for value addition, new product ideas and product differentiations.
14.	Innovation	..	Driven by central R&D.	..	Autonomous and decentralised units.
		..	Science & Technology driven, not customer	..	Cover all functional areas.
		..	Long cycle time	..	Small starts.
		..	Concerned with publication of the findings in journals.	..	Driven by small and short cycle time.
		..	Rushing to patenting	..	Customer/market focused.
				..	More of new products/services impacting the market.
				..	More of new applications impacting the customer
				..	Plant wide activity in every functional area.

EXHIBIT 11.2

Evaluation of Adaptiveness

(a) Only six areas are covered - product, process, quality and safety, product distribution, customer/market, customer service - to serve as illustration. Other areas are also to be covered.

(b) Different aspects covered in each of the six areas are only illustrative and not exhaustive. They need to be enriched and/or modified if need be.

(c) Data need to be furnished as applicable to *each major type product*. Additional information can be given.

A. Product — Name of the product

Sl.No.	Particular	Status as it existed in past			
		5 yrs	3 yrs	1yr	Now
1.	Average cycle time for implementing a major change.				
2.	No. of changes made to:				
	(a) meet market/customer needs.				
	(b) overcome internal difficulties				
	(c) adjust to new raw materials				
	(d) improve safety				
	(f) any other (specify)				
3.	No. of different applications				
4.	No. of new applications				
5.	Name the types of major internal and external failures; and the magnitude for each as defects per unit, per cent rejections, guarantee cost per unit value sold etc.				

B.	Quality And Safety:	Name of the Product			
Sl.No.	Particular	Status as it existed in past			
		5yrs	3yrs	1yr	Now
1.	No. of quality character-isstics.				
2.	No. of quality character-istics as per:				
	(a) BIS Standards				
	(b) ISO Standards				
	(c) Trade practices				
	(d) Customer needs				
	(e) Company standards.				
	(f) Any other specify.				
3.	No. of quality charac-teristics.				
	- Measured				
	- Not measured				
	- Not possible to measure				
4.	No. of safety characteristics				
	- Evaluated				
	- Not evaluated				
	- Not possible to evaluate				
5.	New safety features adopted.				

C. Process	Relevent to product

For each of the major products enumerate the following as applicable to the processes adopted to the product 5 years ago, 3 years, 1 year and now:

— the number of steps involved in the manufacture and simplifications, if any.
— the number of processes employed and the number of those which had no assessment of process capability and the number whose capability are not suitable.
— the number of on-line controls and built in measures to achieve quality.
— the number of on-line measurements of quality characteristics and self adjusting controls.
— Improvements in production, productivity, quality, safety, any others (specify), separately for each of these.

D. Product Distribution

Sl.No.	Particulars		Status as it existed in past			
			5 yrs	3 yrs	1 yr	Now
1.	No. of distributors					
2.	No. of distribution points/ distributor	Ave				
		Max				
		Min				
3.	No.of major customers/ distributor	Ave				
		Max				
		Min				
4.	Sales turnover/distribution point	Ave				
		Max				
		Min				
5.	Types of services offered by distribution to customers.					
6.	Compensation/remuneration rate/distributor					
7.	Incentives to distributor					
8.	Any other (specify).					

E. Customer Service

Enumerate the various types of customer service/facility which have been there during the past 5 yrs, 3 yrs, 1 yr and now.

The following need to be taken note of:

— Customer education
— Ease with which customer can complain
— Speed with which customer gets his grievence redressed.
— Service points
— Service calls made per customer per month/quarter.
— Feed-back on efficiency of customer support systems.
— Repair turn around time.
— Customer contact where, how, frequency, when, why, who.
— Customers' assessment of the quality of customer service as per "discriminating customers".
— Measures taken to improve.
— Any other (specify)

F. Customer/Market		Name of the Product			
Sl.No.	Particulars	Status as it existed in past			
		5 yrs	3 yrs	1 yr	Now
1.	No. of customers				
2.	No. of new customers				
3.	Market share				
4.	Sales volume/value (specify units).				
5.	Per cent of sales value/volume by (2).				
6.	Sales volume through - "commodity", general market - Special segments - "Niche" market - Custom built - Any other (specify).				
7.	*Name the complaints on product from 'discriminating customers'. (a) performance (b) appeal (c) defects (d) any other (other).				

* Qunatitative estimate in terms of number of incidence per unit-sold needs to be given, if available or possible to estimate.

EXHIBIT 11.3

Organic Factors to Strengthen Innovation

Sl.No.	Organic factor & brief description	Purpose
1	2	3
1.	"Stability" in terms of conviction, consensus, commitment, vision and trust.	* To meet effectively "instability" induced by the ever changing environment. * To take risky decisions without fear and reservation. * To change rules, regulations procedures to be more responsive, purposeful and result oriented.
2.	"Love of product, process and services (pps)	* When "pps" get afflicted with defects/failures, to look upon them as "diseases" which need to be immediately cared for, investigated, cured and prevented from occurring. * To build resistance in "pps" through updating, changing, modifying, replacing them by better ones instead of allowing them to get obsolete by a competitor. * To be more responsive, sensitive, proactive to meet fast the changing needs of customers and market.

Contd.

1	2	3
3.	'Understanding', 'Partnership' 'Alliances' as 'Building Blocks', of relationship instead of the traditional ones that are 'legalistic and contractual' 'Adversial and confrontational'.	* To have a workforce prepared to change to meet the 'change' for achieving stability of the enterprise. * To have suppliers who stand by enterprise to keep up its commitment in terms of quantity, quality timely delivery and togetherness to solve problems. * To have loyalty of customers on sound and lasting basis.
4.	Through 'variety' and 'diversity' conquer volume.	* To cater to tiny fragments of consumer markets. ** To move away from 'high volume in few types' mind set. ** To move away from the 'commodity' mind-set.
5.	Precept of "Sweeper I am, Sweeping is sacred" replacing centralised bureaucratic, cubicle located, personal secretary routed style of management through circulars, notes, frozen reports and committees.	* To be in close touch with the ground conditions - shop floor. bazar, suppliers' plant, customers unit etc. - where the 'action' takes place.
6.	Love of change, welcome change, adopt change instead of fearing, resisting and shying away from change.	* To have the verbs build, try, move, establish as the guiding posts of the enterprise. * To survive and succeed as a meaningful and purposeful enterprise in economical as well as societal terms.

12

CONCLUSION

"Change is the only constant". No institution can escape, avoid, confront change. It can do so to become ineffective, irrelevant and possibly even to face extinction.

Hence change has to be used as a productive resource by being adaptive and responsive, and on both being faster than the competitors to ensure survival and success. These depend on the innovative and entreprenurial abilities of an enterprise.

Concepts and tasks described in this book can be used with advantage by any enterprise to manage its innovation effectively and thus ensure its economic prosperity and meaningful existence to society.

BIBLIOGRAPHY

Books

A.J. Harman and A.J. Alexander, "Technological innovation by firms", Rand Report No. R-2237 NSF (1977).

Alvin Toffler, "The Adaptive Corporation", Pan Book Ltd., (1985).

Craig R. Hickman and Michael A. Silva, 'Creating Excellence', New American Library, New York (1984).

Dennis Gabor, "Innovations" Scientific, "Technological and Social", Oxford University Press (1970).

H. James Harrington, "The improvement process", McGraw-Hill International Management Series (1987).

Harvard Business Review, "The Management of technological innovation", (1986).

J.M. Juran, "Juran on leadership for quality", The Free Press, A division of Macmillan Inc., New York (1989).

J.M. Juran, "Juran on Planning for Quality", The Free Press, A Division of Macmillan Inc., New York (1988).

John Naisbitt and Patrice Aburdene, "Mega Trends 2000", Pan Books Ltd. (1990).

John S. Rydz, "Managing Innovation", Ballinger Publishing Company (1986).

Kaoru Ishikawa, "Guide to Quality Control", Asian Productivity Organisation (1976).

Mark H. Mc Cormack, "The 110% Solution", Random House (1991).

Mark H. Mc Cormack, "What they do not teach you at Harvard Business School," Bantom Books (1986).

Michael J Baker (Ed), "Industrial Innovation : technology, policy, diffusion", Macmillan Press (1979).

N. Graig Smith, "Morality and the market", Rout Ledge (1990).

N.S. Sreenivasan, "Management of Safety Concepts and Tasks", IDL Chemicals Ltd. (1984).

Nancy S. Portman, "Innovation and Market Structure", Ballinger Publishing Co., (1987).

Peter F Drucker, "People and Performance - the best of Peter Drucker on Management", Allied Publishers (P) Ltd., (1978).

Peter F. Drucker, "Innovation and Entreprenuership", Pan Books Ltd (1986).

Peter F. Drucker, "Management Tasks, Responsibilities and Practices", Allied Publishers (P) Ltd (1982).

Peter F. Drucker, "Managing in Turbulent Times", Allied Publishers (P) Ltd, (1980).

Peter F. Drucker, "The effective executive", Allied Publishers (P) Ltd. (1972).

Peter F. Drucker, "The Practice of Management", Pan Book Ltd (1972).

Rober L. Khun (Ed-in-chief), "Hand book for creative and innovative managers", McGraw-Hill Book (0.1988).

Shigeru Mizuno, "Managing for Quality Improvement", Productivity Press (1988).

Thomas J. Peters, Robert H. Waterman, "In search for excellence", Harper and Row (1982).

Tom Peters and Nancy Austin, "A Passion for Excellence", Fontane Paper back (1986).

Tom Peters, "Thriving on chaos", Pan Book Ltd. (1989).

Veronica Mole and D. Elliot, "Enterprising Innovation", Frances Pinter (1987).

William Davis, "The innovators", Ebury Press, London (1990).

Articles

R&D Management Series Part I and II Reprints from *Harvard Business Review* (HBR).

"Managing Technological Innovation" Donald R. Schoen, *Harvard Business Review* (HBR) May-June 1969.

"Managing Innovation" controlled chaos, James Brian Quinn *Harvard Business Review*, May-June 1985. No.3

"Product liability" – "Challenger to quality" N.S. Sreenivasan and V. Narayana, *The QR Journal*, 1982.

"Thoughts" on managing "Solid Citizen", "Sniper" and "Dead Wood", N.S. Sreenivasan, *Personnel Today*, Oct-Dec. 1986.

"Managing Quality" – "certain new dimensions and perspectives" N.S. Sreenivasan, "*The QR Journal*", Jan. 1989.

A Managerial concept to the needs of the day "Sweeper Iam, Sweeping is sacred" N.S. Sreenivasan, "*Modern Management*" Nov 87 – April 88.

"Understanding of Innovation Process – a few thoughts" N.S. Sreenivasan, Ibid, Vol. 7 1989.

"Time Element" in innovation activity – a few concepts and tasks". N.S. Sreenivasan, Ibid Vol VI, 1990.

"The business of innovation" "An interview with Paul Cook". *Harvard Business Review* (HBR) March – April, 1990.

"Focus of quality management activities – an apprisal, N.S. Sreenivasan, "*The QR Journal*" September, 1990.

"Filling the need for speed" Tom Peters, *World Executive Digest* Jan 1991.

Book review "The art of the long view by Peter Schwartz", *Fortune*, July, 1991.

INDEX